Theories of Culture in Postmodern Times

To remember

Charles and Cecilia Wagley

Theories of Culture in Postmodern Times

Marvin Harris

ALTAMIRA
PRESS

A Division of Sage Publications, Inc.
Walnut Creek • London • New Delhi

For information address:

AltaMira Press
A Division of Sage Publications, Inc.
1630 North Main Street, Suite 367
Walnut Creek, CA 94596
explore@altamira.sagepub.com
www.altamirapress.com

SAGE Publications Ltd.
6 Bonhill Street
London EC2A 4PU
United Kingdom

SAGE Publications India Pvt. Ltd.
M-32 Market
Greater Kailash 1
New Delhi 110 048

PRINTED IN THE UNITED STATES OF AMERICA

Library of Congress Cataloging-in-Publication Data

Harris, Marvin. 1927–
      Theories of culture in postmodern times / Marvin Harris.
         p.   cm.
      Includes bibliographical references and index.

      ISBN 0-7619-9020-8 (cloth)–ISBN 0-7619-2021-6 (pbk.)
      1. Culture. 2. Ethnology—Philosophy. 3. Anthropology—Philosophy. I. Title.
GN357.H39 1999
306-ddc21

                                                                98-40132
                                                                CIP

99   00   01   02   03   04   05   06   07   10   9   8   7   6   5   4   3   2   1

Production and Editorial Services: David Featherstone
Editorial Management: Jennifer R. Collier
Cover Design: Joanna Ebenstein

Contents

About the Author

MARVIN HARRIS was a member of the faculty of Columbia University's Department of Anthropology from 1953 to 1980, and chairman there from 1963 to 1966. Since 1980, he has been Graduate Research Professor at the University of Florida. Harris has done fieldwork in Brazil, Mozambique, India, and East Harlem.

Of his seventeen books, the most influential are *The Rise of Anthropological Theory: A History of Theories of Culture* (1968); *Culture, People, Nature* (seven editions); *Cows, Pigs, Wars, and Witches: Riddles of Culture* (1974); *Cannibals and Kings* (1977); *Cultural Materialism: The Struggle for a Science of Culture* (1979); and *Our Kind* (1989). Harris's books have been translated into sixteen languages. In 1991, *The Rise of Anthropological Theory* was designated a Social Science Citation Classic.

Harris is past chair of the General Anthropology Division of the American Anthropological Association and the organization's Distinguished Lecturer for 1991.

Preface and Acknowledgments

This year is the thirtieth since the publication of *The Rise of Anthropological Theory: A History of Theories of Culture*, known by friend and foe alike as RAT. I had hoped to mark the occasion by writing a new edition, but that task proved to be too ambitious. The present volume is a more modest project, best described as a sketch of the themes and issues that need to be addressed after three decades of intellectual warfare down among the anthropologi.

I must confess that the turn theory has taken—away from science-oriented processual approaches and toward an "anything goes" postmodernism—has been far more influential than I thought would be possible as I looked ahead from the end of the 1960s. So influential, indeed, that I was tempted to call this volume FAT—the Fall of Anthropological Theory.

But the "pomos'" victory is far from total and certainly not permanent. There are increasing signs that the influence of interpretationism, ethnopoetics, and other "crit lit" approaches to culture has peaked. I hope this volume will help to push the pendulum back toward the science-oriented side. (Let the grinches who stole culture give it back.)

This is not to say that a resurgence of science-oriented theories will necessarily be the *summum bonum* of post-postmodern times. There is also the problem of the kind of sciencing that is taking place. Here we encounter something just as unexpected and disturbing as "anything goes" interpretationism or ethnopoetics: a militant renaissance of various social-Darwinist, raciological, racist, and other biologized approaches that openly call for the end of social science as we know it.

From the vantage point of the late sixties, who could have foreseen the return, in the late nineties, of the attempt to measure racial differences by means of intelligence tests? Or that people would still be using IQ scores as an excuse for tolerating poverty and inequality, even though no one knows what IQ tests measure or how to identify a biologically valid race or provide a count of how many races there actually are. Nor are raciology and racism still popular only among the dominating majorities. With their claims of physical and moral superiority, a hyped-up search for roots and ancestors, and an insistence that they alone have the authority and the competence to understand their cultures and to write their true history, the dominated minorities are often among the worst offenders.

At the same time, nineteenth-century attempts to use Darwinian biology to explain cultural differences and similarities have come full circle. These efforts at biologizing culture gyrate around the great god's natural selection and reproductive success. Yet everyone knows (or should know) that the most distinctive attribute of culture is precisely its plasticity and its ability to evolve independently of changes in the genome.

Additional theoretical issues, equally important, also receive attention in the chapters that follow. These include the definition of culture, the indispensible emic/etic distinction, the struggle to preserve behavior as a component of the cultural domain, the elusive Holy Grail of holism, and the processes responsible for macrocultural evolution.

One may legitimately wonder if the chapters here share a unifying logic that merits their being joined together in a single book. Of course, all of these issues are presided over by the epistemological and theoretical principles of cultural materialism, and in that sense they obviously belong together. But more specifically, the chapters belong together because they deal with a central series of intellectual blockages that must be cleared away before we can begin to reconstruct a viable science of culture amid the ruins of postmodernism.

Let me take this opportunity to thank the many wonderful colleagues and former students of mine who have directly or indirectly helped me to write this book. I am also grateful for having had the opportunity to benefit from the vision and skills of the people of AltaMira Press.

Marvin Harris
Cranberry Island, Maine

Part I

Conceptualizing Culture

Chapter 1

What Is (Are) Culture(s)?

DEFINITIONS

The one dependable ingredient in anthropological definitions of culture is a negative one: culture is not what you get when you study Shakespeare, listen to classical music, or take courses in art history. Beyond that negative, confusion reigns. For some anthropologists, culture consists of the overarching values, motives, and moral-ethical rules and meanings that are a part of a social system. For others, culture embraces not only values and ideas, but the entire set of institutions that humans live by. Some anthropologists see culture as consisting exclusively of learned ways of thinking and behaving, while others emphasize genetic influences on the repertory of cultural traits. Finally, some see culture as consisting exclusively of thoughts or ideas, while others maintain that culture consists of thoughts and ideas plus associated activities. My own view is that a culture is the socially learned ways of living found in human societies and that it embraces all aspects of social life, including both thought and behavior.

As to the mix of genetic versus learned influences that shapes particular cultural traits, I regard that as an empirical question. It seems incontrovertible, however, that the great majority of cultural traits are overwhelmingly shaped by socially mediated learning. More about this point later on. Let us first resolve the question of whether culture should be defined as consisting of ideas alone or of ideas and behavior together.

EMES

William Durham (1992) has forcefully defended the ideational definition of culture, insisting that a distinction must be drawn between culture and human behavior. Durham is not alone; a majority of contemporary anthropologists holds that culture consists exclusively of shared and socially transmitted ideational or mental entities, such as values, ideas, beliefs and the like, "in the minds of human beings" (1991:3). Durham consolidates these mind-things under the umbrella term *meme*, a word invented by Richard Dawkins (1976). For Durham, the meme is the fundamental unit of information that is stored in the brain, transmitted through social learning, and acted upon by the selective forces of cultural evolution.

I do not regard the extirpation of behavior from culture as a mere definitional foible; rather, it implicates certain fundamental theoretical differences between two ways of framing the anthropological enterprise. In the ideational perspective, the relationship between memes and behavior encrypts a definite paradigmatic commitment, namely that ideas determine behavior. Ideas in our minds guide behavior. It is an asymmetric relationship. Memes serves as a "guide" for behavior, but behavior does not serve as a guide for memes. Culture is "the fabric of meaning in terms of which human beings interpret their experience and guide their action" (Geertz 1973:144–5).

Let us suppose for the moment that ideas guide behavior but behavior does not guide ideas. Why should this subordination of behavior to ideas lead to the exclusion of behavior from the concept of culture? One familiar explanation relies on the argument that behavior is too complex, unstructured, and indefinite to serve as the foundation of cultural studies. As argued by Ward Goodenough (1964:39), "the great problem of a science of man is how to get from the objective world of materiality, with its infinite variability, to the subjective world of form as it exists in what, for lack of a better term, we must call the minds of our fellow man."

Anthropologist Oswald Werner (1973:288) offered a similar reason for extirpating behavior from culture. Ideas are forever, but behavior is transient: "Behavior is ephemeral," a mere epiphenomenon of the ideas that underly history. Moreover, behavior is unpredictable for it is subject to "the state of the actor, such as his sobriety, tiredness, or drunkenness" and additional factors some of which "are surely chance."

As we try to understand such views, it may be helpful to identify their philosophical pedigree. The ultimate source of the ideationalist position derives from Plato, for whom the active material world consists of unreal shadows of the ideas that lie behind them. This makes ideas the only entities worthy of study. It has always seemed obvious to me that, contra contemporary Platonists, all fields of study contain components that are infinitely variable. Our job as scientists is to find order in what appears to be disordered. In any event, as will be shown in a moment, the ideationalists have got it wrong. The alleged greater orderliness of mental events is a figment of the imagination (itself a well-known source of cognitive complexity).

Durham takes a somewhat different approach to the stricture against including behavior as well as memes in the definition of culture. The problem, he argues, is that "the conceptual phenomena of culture are only one guiding force of several that may influence the nature and form of behavior" (1991:4). Other guiding forces, such as genes and features of the environment, also influence the nature and form of human behavior. In defining culture, therefore, one must take care not to confuse the effects of learning with the effects of genetic or environmental factors. The way to avoid such confusion is to keep behavior out of the definition of culture. But why can't the same reasoning be applied to memes? Surely one's ideas are also guided by genetic and environmental influences. Genetic predispositions—biopsychological needs and drives in an older terminology—influence the form and content of people's thoughts as well as their behaviors, with the qualification that such constraints and propensities have become weaker, less numerous, and less precise with the evolution of hominid intellectual capabilities.

Some degree of genetic preconditioning probably underlies the widespread (but not universal) belief that a smile is a friendly greeting, or that sweet things are good to eat. If these mixed learned-ideational-genetic memes are acceptable as cultural entities, why deny that mixed learned-genetic socially transmitted behaviors are also a part of culture? Like the act of smiling at the sight of a friend (instead of crying, as the Tapirape Indians do), or the act of putting sugar in coffee or tea (instead of drinking it unsweetened, as dieters do).

To repeat, the attempt to restrict culture to ideational units is no small quibble, but definitions are useful to the extent that they lead to researchable questions about a set of puzzling events and relationships. Definitions are not to be presented as substitutes for empirical research aimed at testing particular theories. Yet when we define culture as pure idea, and describe ideas as guiding social behavior, we are actually advocating a popular paradigmatic principle whose scientific value is scarcely self-evident. Indeed, from my cultural-materialist perspective, the emphasis on the proposition that ideas guide behavior, but not the reverse, is the mother error of contemporary anthropological theories.

CULTURE AS IDEA *AND* BEHAVIOR

Now let me show why the relationship between the ideational and behavioral components of cultures cannot be reduced to the simple formula, "ideas guide behavior." No doubt our brains get filled with cultural instructions—rules—for behavior. These instructions do not contain only rules for guiding our behavior; they also contain rules for breaking those rules. A favorite example concerns an attempt to state the rules that govern the relationship between fathers and married daughters on the Micronesian Island of Truk, as Ward Goodenough reports (1965).

Fathers there should crouch or crawl if a married daughter is seated; avoid initiating any action in her presence; avoid speaking harshly; honor her requests; and never assault her, regardless of provocation. But Goodenough himself witnessed at least one case of a father who broke all of these rules and who ended up giving his married daughter a good hard

jolt. His explanation for the father's misbehavior was that the daughter
had been caught emerging from an amorous tryst. This behavior broke a
number of rules on its own, thereby permitting the father to follow a set of
contradictory rules. The conclusion one might draw is that the vaunted
simplicity of the Platonic realm exists only in the ideationalists' imagina-
tions. In real life, every rule is surrounded by a penumbra of "except and
unless clauses"—rules for breaking rules—which themselves have rules
for breaking rules ad infinitum. Even thieves, murderers, and other socio-
paths have no problem in justifying their behavior by invoking some rule
for breaking rules. (I am reminded of the famous bank robber, Willie
Sutton, who when asked why he robbed banks, replied "Because that's
where the money is.")

Much evidence exists that the cultural information stored in the brain
contains contradictory instructions. For example, in a study of how Americans conceptualize the family, Janet Keller (1992:61–2) recorded these competing "schema":

Family members should strive for the good of the whole
group
  but
The good of the individual takes precedence over the good
of the whole group.

Family is permanent
  but
Family is always in transition.

Family is a refuge
  but
Family is a place to prepare and rehearse public roles.

Family is nurturant
  but
Family is smothering.

Family is divisive, a cauldron of tension and domination
  but
Family is an opportunity for mutual support and warmth.

Another complexity in the ideas-guide-behavior definition arises from the contradictory behavior that results when large numbers of individuals simultaneously attempt to conform to certain rules. For example, avoidance of human fecal matter is a cardinal rule of Hindu farm families yet hookworm, which is transmitted exclusively through contact with fecal matter, is endemic in certain parts of India. In a study carried out by V. K. Kochar (1976) this paradoxical behavioral result was attributed to the existence of six other rules:

- A spot must be found not too far from the house.
- The spot must provide protection against being seen.
- It must offer an opportunity to see any one approaching.
- It should be near a source of water for washing.
- It must be upwind of unpleasant odors.
- It must not be in a field with growing crops.

Fulfilling all of these rules on a small farm leads to behavior that violates the rule for fecal avoidance, as evidenced in the elevated incidence of hookworm.

Closer to home, traffic jams are another example of the unintended and unforeseen behavioral consequences of aggregate conformity to rules. In my experience, there are no rules specifically concerned with guiding traffic into gridlock. Indeed, the rules that apply to driving are all concerned with maintaining rapid and safe progress toward a destination.

On a still more macro scale, one might ask where the rules are that serve as guides to becoming impoverished or homeless. Presumably, the operative rules are aimed at not becoming a pauper and at not becoming homeless. Competitive application of such rules (e.g., work hard and don't take drugs) may lead one person to success but another to failure, depending on the intensity of effort and also on something as nebulous as "luck." Thus, to explain poverty and homelessness, we need to deal with higher-order systemic processes, rather than with rules.

ANIMAL CULTURES

An additional obvious defect of the ideational definition of culture is the disjuncture it creates between the rudimentary cultural traditions exhibited by chimpanzees and other nonhuman primates and the full-blown repertory of cultural traits characteristic of humans. Chimpanzee traditions consist of the manufacture and use of various tools such as leafless twigs for "anting" and "termiting," the use of rocks to pound open nuts and hard fruits, and the wadding of leaves to make sponges for soaking up drinking water. These behaviors occur in some local groups of the same species and not in others, and they clearly depend on some form of socially mediated learning. Their importance lies in the light they shed on the evolution of the human capacity for culture at a prelinguistic level. One must assume that the behaviors in question are not guided by information stored in the form of memes. (Or do chimpanzees have ideas just like people have?) This returns us to the question of whether behavior in humans is always guided by ideas, and never the other way round.

WHAT GUIDES IDEAS?

Down through the ages, nothing has appeared more certain to untutored, as well as to learned, men and women than the concept that ideas guide behavior. All of our experience conducts us to the same conclusion: activities are under the control of our values, meanings, and intentions. I do not wish to challenge this conviction. We humans attempt to organize our lives in conformity with culturally patterned rules, plans, schemas, scripts, and goals. We do, in fact, carry on a ceaseless and silent internal dialogue for micromanaging our daily affairs, such as getting out of bed in the morning, taking a shower, preparing breakfast, driving to work, sitting at our desk, meeting a friend for lunch, and so forth.

In this narrow theater, the actors can be said to be guided by their ideational scripts. If that was all that transpired in human social life, both life and the science of culture would be "a piece of cake." As many of us are acutely aware, however, our ideational and behavioral repertories cannot be reduced to a set of stable, permanent programs. Human social life entails ceaseless changes in all its behavioral and ideational sectors, and it is here—in the more or less rapid evolution of cultural repertories—that the ideational approach meets its Waterloo. It is also here, in the medium to long run, that behavior guides ideas—shapes, orients, uproots, tears down, and raises up the nexus of cognitive features that accompany and guide behavior in the short run.

Consider for example, the events leading to the demise of the male-breadwinner, multichild, nuclear family in the United States. The case is well known. Early in the twentieth century, basic rules for marriage and gender roles stipulated that, upon marriage, women had to remove themselves from the paid labor force, become housewives, bear three or more children, and stay married to the same husband for the rest of their lives. The ideas associated with these behaviors were widely and strongly held well into the 1970s. However, the behaviors themselves began to change in the 1950s as women were pushed and pulled into the wage labor force in response to the shift from a smokestack to a service and information economy. The new mode of production placed a premium on a literate, docile, and educated labor force, rendering multichild families unaffordable at middle-class standards of living unless there were two wage earners per household. Married women initially regarded their jobs as temporary stopgap measures; but as their participation in the wage labor force expanded, they began to compete for the better-paying careers. Today, the idea that a woman's role is to stay home, take care of the children, and leave the wage-earning to a husband seems absurd to the majority of American women. Many other ideational shifts in gender roles, sexuality, and family life followed on the behavioral changes that were induced by the shift to a service-and-information mode of production.

As Valerie Oppenheimer shows in her book *Work and the Family*, behavior changed first, and in so doing, gave rise to a whole new set of rules and values:

> There is no evidence that these substantial shifts in
> women's labor force participation were precipitated by
> prior changes in sex role attitudes. On the contrary, they
> lagged behind behavioral changes, indicating that changes
> in behavior have gradually brought about changes in sex
> role norms rather than the reverse. Moreover, the evidence
> clearly indicates that the start of the rapid changes in
> women's labor force behavior greatly preceded the birth of
> the feminist movement. (1982:30)

Explanations of cultural behavior that start from the premise that ideas guide behavior, but not the reverse, are doomed to being dead ends. Such explanations cannot specify any conditions that could account for observed changes in cultural repertoires other than some additional prior ideas. But prior ideas do not constitute a set of constraints that make subsequent ideas predictable. It is not enough to say that an idea is "good to think" or "bad to think." One must be prepared to specify why it is good or bad at a particular time and place. It was not difficult for women to think about finding employment away from home; what was difficult was the materialization of such thoughts in behavior. There is nothing inherently more difficult in thinking that men should dominate women than in thinking that women should dominate men. The difficulty comes when one sex rather than the other gains a political advantage based on power differences.

What is the force that compels the Iroquois to think that descent is to be reckoned exclusively through maternal relationships? To Jews and Moslems, pork is forbidden. "This idea is part of their religion," we say. But why do these religions have such an idea? Only when behavior is brought into the picture and rooted in material conditions can we understand the forces that compel the thinking of certain thoughts rather than others.

Clearly, behavior and ideas must be seen as elements in a feedback relationship. In the short run, ideas do guide behavior; but in the long run, behavior guides and shapes ideas. I will have more to say about this relationship in the chapters to come. But one additional claim put forward by ideationalists needs to be cleared up first.

No Consensus

William Durham (1992:3) maintains that the exclusively ideational definition of culture represents a "new and hopeful consensus" in anthropology. I concede that over the last fifty years, commencing with Alfred Kroeber's surrender to Talcott Parsons's ideational construction of social systems (Kroeber and Parsons 1958; Harris 1975), the majority of anthropologists have come to accept an exclusively ideational definition of culture. Many of the more popular American introductory textbooks have adopted "the-guide-to-behavior-but-not-behavior" definition. Conrad Kottak's (1991:17) definition, for example, contains the phrase, "traditions and customs that govern behavior." Likewise, William Haviland (1993:29) states, "Culture consists of the abstract values, beliefs, and perceptions of the world that lie behind people's behavior, and which are reflected in their behavior."

One can scarcely conclude, however, that the majority view has passed into consensus. An inspection of current textbooks quickly turns up dissenters such as Serena Nanda (1991:52), who writes that "The term *culture* . . . describes the specifically human type of learned behavior in which arbitrary rules and norms are so important." Melvin and Carol Ember (1990:17) go further and flatly reject the claim that a majority of anthropologists have banished behavior from culture. They assert instead that "To most anthropologists, culture encompasses the learned behaviors, beliefs, attitudes, values, and ideals that are characteristic of a particular society or population."

Whether or not there is a consensus on the exclusively ideational nature of culture, the question remains as to the scientific value of such a definition. Surprisingly little attention has been devoted toward explaining why the purely ideational definition is a good thing. After all, no one has sought to define culture as exclusively behavioral. Wouldn't it be best to accept both ideas and behavior as our starting point?

Chapter 2

Emics and Etics

Having discussed the importance and legitimacy of both ideas and behavior in the definition of culture, we are ready to examine another fundamental epistemological distinction, that between emics and etics.

Because of the uniquely human capacity to provide descriptions and interpretations of our own experiences, cultures may be studied from two perspectives: one oriented to the participants' point of view, and the other oriented to the observers' point of view. Participant-oriented studies result in emic descriptions and interpretations. Observer-oriented studies result in etic descriptions and interpretations.

More precisely, emic statements describe social systems of thought and behavior whose phenomenal distinctions, entities, or "things" are built up out of contrasts and discriminations sensed by the participants themselves as similar or different, real, meaningful, significant, or appropriate. An emic statement can be proven wrong if it can be shown that it contradicts the participants' sense that entities and events are similar or different, real, meaningful, significant, or appropriate.

Etic statements, on the other hand, depend upon phenomenal distinctions judged appropriate by a community of scientific observers. Etic statements cannot be proven wrong if they do not conform to the participants' sense of what is significant, real, meaningful, or appropriate. They

I wish to acknowledge that critiques offered by Brian Ferguson compelled me to rethink aspects of the problem discussed in this chapter.

can only be proven wrong by the failure of empirical evidence gathered by observers to support the statements in question.

These terms—emic and etic—which derive from the distinction between phonemic and phonetic aspects of languages, were invented by the linguist Kenneth Pike. Although the terms have been adopted by substantial numbers of anthropologists, it is not clear that all contemporary users actually mean what Pike means by emic and etic. The differences between myself and Pike center on the role that etics play in the development of a science of culture.

In the first edition of his three-volume *Language in Relation to a Unified Theory of the Structure of Human Behavior* (1954, 1955, 1960), Pike seemed to be proposing a sharp separation between emic and etic approaches. But it subsequently became clear that, for Pike, phonetic descriptions represent the distillation of the cumulative knowledge of phonemic systems found in various languages and cultures around the world. Because of its ultimate dependence on prior and current emic analysis, a phonetic description, according to Pike, is thus far from being sharply separable from emics as in my use of the terms. For Pike, *etics* denotes:

> an approach by an outsider to an inside system, in which
> the outsider brings his own structure and partly super-
> imposes his observations on the inside view, interpreting
> the inside in reference to his outside starting point.
> (Pike 1986b)

Thus etics, for Pike, are in part observers' emics incorrectly applied to a foreign system. It is only a small step from this position to the conclusion that observers' etics are just another variety of emics: that "the nature of things is emic not etic" (Levi-Strauss 1972:13). Such a conclusion endows participants with a more privileged form of knowledge than the trained observers and constitutes an open invitation to epistemological chaos.

It is the existence of a community of scientific observers that prevents the mind-numbing collapse of etics into emics. The members of this community share in common a commitment to a set of epistemological and theoretical principles and methodologies acquired during a more or less rigorous and lengthy training period. To reduce etics to the emics of the observer, therefore, is in effect to challenge the legitimacy of science as a special way of knowing. The observers have no recourse but to defend science against those who are hostile to it. It is the trained and well-informed anthropologists and other social and behavioral scholars and scientists who make the social sciences possible. Our "emics," applied to the study of sociocultural phenomena, are a very special kind of emics because they are uniquely responsive to the task of building a science of society and culture. It is for this reason that the emics of the observers must be categorically distinguished from the emics of the participants, and that is why we need the term *etics* as well as *emics*.

The current resistance to science and etics (Kuznar 1997) is closely related to the struggle of participants who are emerging from oppressive colonial and neocolonial subordination and who demand exclusive control over the interpretation, description, and reconstruction of their lifeways and histories. Anthropologists seeking access to the world of the participants recoil in horror at the prospect of being identified as arrogant expropriators of other people's matri-patrimony—as stealers of cultures.

The only solution to this conundrum is for the community of science-oriented anthropologists to pursue its quest for understanding by employing both emic and etic approaches. I will have more to say in later chapters about the moral-political issues raised by native participants' and their politically correct opposition to being studied by nonparticipant scientists.

WHOSE COMMUNITY OF OBSERVERS?

Before moving on, let me deal with the vexing problem that surrounds the concept of a "community of scientific observers." We are all aware of the fact that there is not just a single community of such observers. Setting aside scholary groups who are frankly opposed to science-oriented approaches, there remain a number of alternative paradigmatic options. Here

we encounter evolutionists and antievolutionists, materialists and idealists, ideationalists and behaviorists, emicists and eticists, and so forth (not
to mention older approaches that have come and gone). This situation
prompted Thomas Kuhn, the father of paradigms, to regard the social sciences as "preparadigmatic." Thus, "community of observers" need not mean
the totality of science-oriented researchers; rather, it refers to researchers
who agree about certain minimum criteria for developing scientific information about a particular domain of existence (e.g., criteria of replicability,
testability, parsimony, scope, etc.). At a minimum, a community of social
science observers has to agree that the distinction between observer and
observed is real. As for the number of observers in the community, there is
no fixed quantity. *In extremis*, one could argue that it only takes a handful
of people to make a scientific community, (although when there are only
one or two like-minded members, something is obviously amiss).

SUBJECTIVE/OBJECTIVE

Before one decides to add neologisms such as emic and etic to an already
over-burdened dictionary of social science–speak, a search should be made
for terms that are already in use and synonymous.

One candidate is the opposition between subjective and objective.
My dictionary (Webster's Third) defines subjective as "lacking in reality or
substance; illusory, fanciful." And it defines objective as "publicly or
intersubjectively observable or verifiable especially by scientific methods."
Thus *etic* is very close in meaning to *objective*; but *subjective* does not match
with *emic*. The problem is that emic descriptions can be objective as well
as subjective. Indeed, some of the most rigorously scientific projects carried out in the social sciences have been directed at discovering participants' categorizations of plants, animals, colors, and kin terms. In research
in Brazil, my colleagues and I have tried to carry out scientific experi-
ments involving a split census, controlled drawings, tests for significance,
etc., to arrive at an understanding of how Brazilians categorize race-color

differences. These are clearly emic studies because they are concerned with the meaning of race-color categories as understood by the participants (Harris et al. 1993).

To clarify the differences between subjective/objective and emic/etic, I suggest that we use subjective/objective to refer to operations from the point of view of whether they satisfy the general epistemological canons of scientific inquiry and scientific theory. That is, they must be public, replicable, testable, broad in scope, and parsimonious. Etic operations are necessarily science-and-observer-oriented, but an emic operation (e.g., eliciting race-color terms) can be carried out subjectively or objectively. Much to my dismay, anthropologists continue to equate objective and scientific exclusively with etics (e.g., Cassidy 1987:318). But emic studies of cognitive categories routinely satisfy the criteria of scientific inquiry, even though one might prefer that such studies would result in more broadly applicable theories.

Insider/Outsider

Also much to my dismay, the book *Emics and Etics*, edited by Thomas Headland (1991), bears the subtitle *The Insider-Outsider Debate*. In my contribution to that volume, I tried to demonstrate the nonequivalence of insider/outsider with emic/etic. To repeat the argument, this distinction lacks clarity because it does not specify whether the outsider's point of view leads to emic or etic knowledge based respectively on emic or etic operations. In my Brazilian ethnographic research, I was always an outsider whether or not I was gathering etic or emic data. Similarly, one can be an outsider (like a member of a rival gang) and have no interest in a scientific-etic description of the gang's turf. Used in this manner, the distinction between insider and outsider does not come to grips with the epistemologically salient meaning of the emic/etic contrast.

Cognized/Operational

As defined by Rappaport (1984:236–7), the operational model is essentially what I mean by etics, but the cognized model is not isomorphic with emics:

> The operational model is that which anthropologists
> construct through observation and measurement of
> empirical entities, events, and material relationships. He/
> (she) takes this model to represent, for analytic purposes,
> the physical world of the group he/(she) is studying.

In contrast, the cognized model "is the model of the environment conceived by the people who act in it."

The problem here is the lack of specificity concerning how one knows about the cognized model as conceived by the participants. As I have already indicated, there are both emic and etic operations for obtaining knowledge about rules, plans, goals, and values, and they can result in contradictory descriptions of what is going on inside the participant's brain.

Mental/Behavioral

The mental/behavioral model has the same problem as cognized/operational since it does not specify whether it is the participants' or the observer's sense of what the participants think and do that is being described.

Other related oppositions such as "folk systems/analytical systems" (Bohannon 1963:12), "structural/ecological" (Johnson 1982:413), and "experience near/experience distant" (Geertz 1976:223) suffer from one or another or all of the ambiguities previously mentioned. The existence and frequent use of all of these oppositions suggest that we are dealing with a fundamental epistemological quandary that will not go away by itself and that will require serious and prolonged discussion before it can be resolved.

EMIC/ETIC VS. MENTAL/BEHAVIORAL

In formulating the emic/etic distinction prior to 1979, I failed to see that the mental/behavioral distinction was not congruent with emics/etics. Hence, emics were seen as referring exclusively to events taking place in the participant's brain while etics were seen as referring exclusively to actonics (i.e., body motions and their environmental effects). It is clear, however, that social science literature is, in fact, filled with statements that purport to represent a participant's thoughts, intentions, values, criteria of appropriateness, categories, and mental and emotional states, but which are based essentially on etic rather than emic operations.

French structuralism is a prolific source of such statements, as when ethnographers claim that a series of binary contrasts, such as men versus women, up versus down, and right versus left, derive from a common cognitive template—culture versus nature—even though no participant acknowledges the appropriateness of the postulated contrasts and relationships. (French structuralist Levi-Strauss relied mainly on published collections of myths recorded by others and thus was without benefit of live participants.) More emphatically, even if participants deny that these structural oppositions make sense to them, the observers would not admit that such inferences were invalid.

Psychoanalytic approaches to mental life result in similar statements. On the basis of various verbal and nonverbal cues, analysts infer that the client hates a parent or envies a sibling even though the client may insist that these inferences are inappropriate.

Inferences about mental and emotional states from so-called body language cues and facial expressions possess the same epistemological status: they lead psychologists to make statements about the inner life of participants whose validity does not depend upon testing the participants' sense of appropriateness. Disregard of the participants' sense of appropriateness is also a common feature of Western legal practice, where judges and juries routinely attempt to determine not only if defendants have actually committed a crime, but also if defendants intended to do so with "malice aforethought."

Dead Participants

Historians also are much devoted to making inferences about what was going on in the minds of specific individuals. (What was Abe Lincoln really thinking about when he wrote the Gettysburg Address?) Of course, the fact that historians deal for the most part with persons who are dead greatly complicates their task, but they can compensate for this handicap by perusing various forms of written evidence, ranging from official documents to love letters. Where the written materials are abundant and sufficiently personal, historians may achieve a credible level of both etic and emic accounts of both behavior and thought. We can reasonably believe that Lincoln was assassinated on April 14, 1865, while attending the theater (etics) and that millions of people regarded him as a great man and felt sorrow at his passing (emics).

How "Natives" Think about Captain Cook for Example

The problem confronted by anthropologists who want to describe the content of the minds of dead people is much more severe. Typically, the peoples under study lack writing and leave no record of their thoughts and feelings (except ambiguous traces of their physical presence and some of their activities). Observers are therefore compelled to make inferences based on subjective methods if they seek to examine the content of participants' minds. The perils of such a strategy stand out in the bitter controversy between Marshall Sahlins(1995) and Gananath Obeyesekere (1992) about what was going on in the minds of the Hawaiians when they killed the renowned English explorer Captain James Cook in 1779.

Sahlins maintains that the Hawaiians believed Cook was their god Lono. He based this claim almost entirely on accounts written by European explorers, missionaries, and traders (plus a few modern-day Hawaiian scholars). Cook enjoyed his apotheosis until his ships set sail, encountered damaging winds, and had to return to the Hawaiian harbor. This unanticipated reappearance alarmed the Hawaiian chiefs and priests, who now saw Lono-Cook as threatening their survival. Lono-Cook therefore had to be killed, as foretold in their myths about Lono. Thereupon Cook was "ritually murdered."

According to Obeyesekere, however, the Hawaiians believed that Cook was a chief, not a god. It was the Europeans themselves, not the Hawaiians, who invented and propagated the divinity of Cook. The Hawaiians killed Cook because he had lost his self-control and was trying to take a high-ranking chief as a hostage. At no time were the Hawaiians so naive as to think that Cook and his men were actually gods.

Although Sahlins and Obeyesekere have offered enormous quantities of citations from logs and journals kept by Cook and his ship-board companions and from the reports of every traveler and missionary familiar with the pertinent events, the controversy canot be resolved. We know what the Europeans were thinking, but in the absence of living participants and of documents written by Hawaiians who were alive two hundred years ago, the argument about what the Hawaiians were thinking cannot rise above speculation. The best we can hope for is to agree on what the Europeans thought the Hawaiians were thinking.

EMICS AND ETICS OF BEHAVIOR

Once it is conceded that the domain of mental life can be subjected to etic as well as emic analysis, then the question arises as to whether the domain of behavior—the "behavior stream"—can be subjected to both forms of analysis as well. My answer is affirmative. There is a class of emic descriptions that is concerned with the participant's understanding of the behavioral events that occur (or that have occurred or will occur) in a particular time and place. For example, one can elicit accounts from participants about specific events, such as who was present at a wedding, birth, or funeral; what was said by a politician; how much grain was harvested; or how many calves were killed by a farmer. Again, however, the observers must be prepared for discrepancies and contradictions in the emic and etic versions of the events in question. This category of emics deserves special emphasis because it poses the great questions of informant reliability (cf. Bernard et al. 1984), relativism, and historical truth.

To sum up, the reformulation of the emic/etic distinction to include mental and behavioral qualifiers results in four contrasting modes of ethnographic descriptions: emics of mental life, emics of behavior, etics of mental life, and etics of behavior. As I will show in a moment, failure to make these distinctions subverts our ability to agree on even the most salient ethnographic facts. But first let me clear up another persistent point of confusion.

ARE ETIC AND EMIC ACCOUNTS ALWAYS DIFFERENT?

The emic analysis of languages normally results in statements that convey little meaning or sense of appropriateness to native speakers. Few speakers of English can state the rules governing the formation of plural nouns, for example. Many might deny that the words *cats*, *houses*, and *flags* end with different allomorphs (phonemic variants). Grammatical rules nonetheless have the same epistemological status as phonemes, since the test of their validity, no matter how abstract the formulation, is whether they generate utterances that native speakers recognize as meaningful and appropriate. Such tests, however, are irrelevant for etic analyses, which stand or fall on their contribution to the development of scientific theories about sociocultural phenomena. This does not mean that etic analysis necessarily results in descriptions that are at variance with participants' sense of appropriateness and historical truth. In many domains, but especially in technological processes, emic versions of cultural practices and behavior-stream events correspond closely to etic versions of the same. Allen Johnson studied this problem among Brazilian peasant farmers. He found that elicited rules for planting crops on particular kinds of lands and elicited descriptions of past planting activity sometimes corresponded closely with etically observed behavior. But as Johnson emphasized, the facts of correspondence or noncorrespondence raise equally important questions:

Why are some rules followed while others are broken?
Why do some individuals follow rules while others break
them? Why are some rules and concepts widely shared
while others vary from individual to individual?
(1974:100)

The Rejection of Etics

The reason there are no epistemological distinctions in the social sciences
that fully anticipate emics and etics is that, to this very day, the dominant
paradigms of the social sciences have never accepted the importance, or
even the possibility, of describing human social life in terms of the motions of body parts and their environmental effects (and higher-order structures derived therefrom) as a counterpoint to descriptions of social life
based on elicited intentions, meanings, and values, and hypostatized social groups, statuses, institutions, events, and practices. The doctrine of
the nonadmissibility of etic descriptions has an absolute—shall I say dog-
matic?—finality to it in the writings of leading figures in the history of
sociological and anthropological theory. For example, Talcott Parsons
(1961:32) wrote, "the study of human social behavior necessarily involves
. . . a type of theoretical scheme [that] treats behavior as 'goal-directed,' as
'adaptive,' as 'motivated,' and as guided by symbolic processes." He then
added:

> A major focus of this problem was the "behaviorist"
> controversy of the 1920s. The behaviorist position was a
> major example of reductionism and tended to deny the
> scientific legitimacy of all "subjective" categories, of all
> concepts of "meaning . . ." As in the battles over the status
> of science itself and over empiricism in this area, it can be
> said that the fight is over. Sociological theory today is
> clearly couched in terms of motives, goals, symbols,
> meanings, means and ends, and the like. (1961:32–3)

For anthropologist John Beattie, the battle was over before it began:

> Social relations cannot be intelligibly conceived or
> described apart from the expectations, intentions and
> ideas which they express or imply: *certainly no social
> anthropologist has ever attempted so to describe them.*
> (1968:117; emphasis added)

Parsons's reference to behaviorism in the 1920s has relevance only to paradigms in psychology. The battle in the social sciences to which he alludes was a figment of his imagination. There never were any Pavlovian or Watsonian social scientists. No such battle as Parsons describes was ever fought, precisely because it has always seemed self-evident that the key to human behavior lies in the distinctively human capacity for expressing expectations, intentions, and ideas. Ironically, many cultural anthropologists and archaeologists who are now advocates of interpretationist, postprocessualist, and antipositivist paradigms (e.g., Marcus & Fischer 1986) seem to think that they are promulgating a great intellectual revolution when they call for the "unity of meaning (beliefs) and action" (Hodder 1982:2), or, in the words of Shanks and Tilley (1987:38), assert the "need to distinguish between physical bodily movement which can be accommodated in terms of a naturalist thesis and human actions which cannot be readily assimilated as they involve intentions, choices, dispositions and motivations."

For the record, I need to be equally emphatic. Human behavior not only *can* be described without attempting to infer or elicit intentions, choices, dispositions, and motivations, but such descriptions are *indispensable* in order to allow for the human capacity to lie, obfuscate, forget, and disguise our inner lives; to say one thing and do another; and to produce in the aggregate effects that were not intended by any participant. What is remarkable about the rejection of behaviorist accounts of human social action is its exclusionary and apodictic tone. Nothing quite so totalizing has ever been produced by the materialist camp. We assert only that descriptions of human cultures must distinguish between behavioral and mental accounts and between emic and etic accounts. Cultural materialists do not seek to eliminate emic and mental accounts, but rather to explain the relation of these accounts to behavioral and etic accounts.

Given the well-nigh hegemonic status of emic and mentalist perspectives in contemporary anthropology, advocates of etic and behaviorist perspectives are obliged to consider the absence of those perspectives as a threat to the viability of the entire anthropological undertaking. An example follows.

An Ethnographic Disaster

In a study of Windigo psychosis, an alleged culture-specific mental disorder attributed to Northern Algonkian peoples, Louis Marano (1982:385) found the absence of etic behavioral data to be "an invitation to ethnological disaster."

- The emics of mental life, revealed through ethnographic interviews and verbatim testimony, was that certain people became transformed into powerful monsters—Windigos—and had to be killed to prevent them from satisfying their cannibal urges.
- The emics of the behavior stream was that particular individuals turned into Windigos, attempted to eat their campmates, and were killed in self-defense.
- On the basis of these emic accounts, anthropologists and psychiatrists inferred that Northern Algonkians were prone to a psychosis defined by an irresistible desire to consume human flesh (etics of mental life).
- But the etic behavioral record, largely ignored by Marano's predecessors, clashes with the emics of behavior and the etics of mental life.

Marano could not find cases in which alleged Windigos were actually trying to eat their campmates when they were killed. Instead, alleged Windigos were, for the most part, sick or troublesome individuals who were slain during stressful episodes associated with shortages of game and the spread of epidemic diseases. A complete redefinition of the ethnographic reality now ensues. Etically and behaviorally, the killing of alleged Windigos becomes an instance of a cross-culturally recurrent etic behavioral pattern that Marano calls "triage homicide." This leads, in turn, to a complete up-ending of the etics of mental life: People invoke the threat of Windigo in order to justify the practice of triage homicide.

Sacred Cow Revisited

Marano's analysis leaves us with the question of to what extent there was an elicitable emics of thought and behavior that corresponded to the etic behavioral analysis of the Windigo complex, but that was never elicited simply because the etic behavioral basis for formulating such a question was ignored. This question must now remain unanswered because triage homicide is no longer practiced among contemporary Northern Algonkian peoples. A similar question has been posed, however, regarding my analysis of the sacred cow complex in India.

On the basis of emic and etic data collected during fieldwork in and near Trivandrum, in Kerala state, I formulated the following illustration of the four ethnographic modes, which are described on page 40, relative to the rearing of cattle (Harris 1979:38):

- Emics of mental life: All calves have the right to life.
- Emics of behavior stream: No calves are ever starved to death.
- Etics of mental life: Let the male calves starve to death when feed is scarce.
- Etics of behavior stream: Male calves are regularly starved to death.

Anthropologist James Sebring (1987) challenged the accuracy of my rendering of Hindu farmers' emics. Hindu farmers in Almora District, Uttar Pradesh, told Sebring that they themselves starved some calves to death (emic/behavioral) and that it is proper to do so in order to get the greatest economic values from them (emic/mental). Although Sebring's participants were from a different village and state, I have no reason to doubt that if I had managed to become more intimate with my participants, some of them would have confided that they did in fact cull the unwanted sex and that it was economically necessary for them to do this. Indeed, this is exactly what is implied in the etic/mental modality (mode 3 above) by the formula "Let the male calves starve to death when feed is scarce," which I inferred wholly on the basis of the etics of behavior. Instead of congratulating me for reading the minds of my participants, Sebring launched into an attack on the validity of my emic accounts on the grounds that practical farmers do not believe in the "saintly" idea of cow protection.

In my experience, however, farmers were acutely sensitive to the need to show conformity to "saintly" Hindu prescriptions if for no other reason than that it is illegal, as well as sacrilegious, to slaughter calves. The heart of the matter, as I see it, is that people tend to have alternative emic prescriptions—often contradictory—that can be brought to saliency by comparison with the etic behavioral record. As we saw earlier, participants always have recourse to rules for breaking rules. The road to a better understanding of both emics and etics, therefore, lies through the persistent juxtaposition of emic and etic versions of social life.

THE IMPORTANCE OF ETICS

This is not to say that it is always possible to elicit emic accounts that match up with etic accounts. On the contrary, every culture undoubtedly contains emic constructions whose main function is to prevent people from seeing their behavior in ways that might correspond to etic behavioral descriptions, and it is especially in these domains that ethnography stands or falls on its capacity and its determination to offer etic behavioral accounts.

Let me illustrate this point with the practice of indirect infanticide among the women of Alto do Cruzeiro, in northeast Brazil, as reported by Nancy Scheper-Hughes. Alto do Cruzeiro women said that out of 251 deaths between birth and five years, 76 had been caused by *doença da criança* (child sickness) or *fraqueza* (weakness). From the emic perspective, these are incurable afflictions that no amount of intervention by the infant's mother can remedy: "the cause of death is a perceived deficiency [emics of the behavior stream] in the child, not a deficiency in the mother" (Scheper-Hughes 1987:198). However, from an etic behavioral perspective, the inevitability of these deaths is dependent on the selective neglect that is forced upon pauperized mothers who on average experience 9.5 pregnancies and have to cope with 4.5 living children. According to Scheper-Hughes:

> It became painfully apparent that Alto mothers were often describing the symptoms of severe malnutrition and gastro-enteric illness further complicated by their own selective inattention. Untreated diarrheas and dehydration contributed to the baby's passivity, his or her disinterest in food, and developmental delays. High fevers often produced the fit-like convulsions that mothers feared as harbingers of permanent madness or epilepsy. Because these hungry and dehydrated babies are so passive and uncomplaining, their mothers can easily forget to attend to their needs, and can distance themselves emotionally from what comes to appear as an unnatural child, an angel of death that was never meant to live. Many such babies are left alone in their hammocks while their mothers are out working, and not even a sibling or a neighbor woman is within earshot when their feeble cries signal a final crisis, and so they die alone and unattended. (1987:198)

Could a corresponding emic account ever be elicited from the participants? This seems highly unlikely. Needless to say, not only is infanticide a capital crime in Brazil, but the women of Alto do Cruzeiro regard it as such. When a young mother who would not let nature take its course killed her infant and one-year-old baby outright, she was universally reviled as a beast and unnatural creature.

The struggle to prevent anthropology from abandoning its etic accountability is no mere disputation about epistemological minutia. Etic data concerning selective neglect and indirect infanticide (B. Miller 1981; Scrimshaw 1984) have implications for policy decisions that are quite different from those resulting from emic data. Thus, withholding contraceptive information and technology in combination with the interdiction of medical abortion frequently has the unintended consequence of promoting the practice of homicide. Families overburdened with more children than they can rear must make choices concerning the allocation of resources that result in premature deaths. From an emic point of view common in the United States, abortion is the murder of the fetus; from an etic point of view, the prohibition of abortion often leads to the murder of an infant or child in disadvantaged classes and countries. Adherence to the dogma of the unity of form and meaning in human action in this instance, as in many others, amounts to a cover-up of unintended consequences that adversely affect the lives of millions of people.

ETIC ACCOUNTS NEEDED FOR PREDICTION

I am not prepared to say that unintended consequences are more common than intended ones, especially since, as I have already noted, intentions may be redesigned post facto to fit occasions. I am prepared to say, however, that the bigger the social problem, the less likely that it can be accounted for by emic intentions and the more likely that there are no elicitable emic accounts that match the etic behavioral accounts. Consider, for example, the problems of depletion and pollution. I think we can safely say that the designers of automobiles, factories, power stations, and refrigerators did not intend to create gridlock, smog, acid rain, holes in the ozone layer, or the greenhouse effect, all of which have profoundly influenced our everyday social lives. In the same way, there are no salient intentional emic prescriptions in the United States for making people poor and homeless. When employers lay off their workers, their intention is to make money, not to create an underclass. Even the sheriff who carries out an eviction order intends not to make people homeless, but merely to make them vacate a particular house or apartment. Similarly, people who argue on behalf of owning handguns simply intend to defend themselves, not to increase the homicide rate.

~

Underlying the frequency with which intentions and social consequences do not match is the fact that much of social life, even in band and village societies, is a product of intersecting and often conflicting meanings and intentions. In chiefdoms and states, these intersections and conflicts often take the form of a struggle for power between men and women, social classes, factions, and ethnic, religious, and racial groups, the outcome of which cannot conceivably be predicted or retrodicted even with the most perfect knowledge of the emics of the participants (Harris 1975). It is only through etic accounts of behavioral events that unintended outcomes, or outcomes intended but dependent on differential amounts of power, can be predicted or retrodicted. Moreover, the importance of etic behavioral accounts necessarily increases with the span of time over which one seeks explanations for sociocultural differences and similarities.

For anthropologists who are concerned with the evolution of culture from remote times to the present, there is no alternative to etic descriptions. As previously discussed, the absence of written records as well as of living informants from prehistory simply precludes the collection of reliable emic data. I am aware of course of a resurgence of interest among archaeologists in "the meaningful construction of social acts" (Hodder 1982:22), but alas, these reconstructions necessarily represent the etics of mental life whose correspondence with emic structures must forever remain untestable.

Chapter 3

The Nature of Cultural Things

Recognition of the emic/etic and mental/behavioral options positions us for resolving (or at least confronting) a long-standing dilemma of the social sciences: the relationship between the individual and society and the ontological status of supraindividual sociocultural entities and forces.

METHODOLOGICAL HOLISM AND METHODOLOGICAL INDIVIDUALISM

Two opposing camps, the methodological holists and the methodological individualists, can be discerned. Methodological holism has an intellectual pedigree that extends back through Emile Durkheim, Karl Marx, Herbert Spencer, Auguste Comte, and ultimately to Thomas Hobbes's "artificial animal," the "great Leviathan called the Commonwealth or the State." As we shall see in chapter 10, there are several other varieties of holism that need to be distinguished but which are not pertinent to the definition of cultural entities and sociocultural systems.

Methodological holists contend that sociocultural life constitutes a level of phenomena that is outside and beyond that of the individuals who are subjected to the phenomena in question. In Durkheim's (1938:13) formulation, the domain of the social consists of social things or "facts" which are "capable of exercising on the individual an external restraint . . . existing in its own right independent of its individual manifestations."

In anthropology, the supraindividual holist approach had its strongest defenders in Leslie White and Alfred Kroeber. They postulated (borrowing from Herbert Spencer) a culturological or "superorganic" level of phenomena that could not be reduced to the level of the thoughts and behavior of individuals. (Kroeber recanted his support for this position late in his career [Harris 1968:333].) Thus, society and culture and their constituent parts exist prior to individuals, who have little choice but to participate in the institutions and to learn the roles that society has prepared for them.

Methodological individualism, on the other hand, holds that social and cultural phenomena are to be explained solely in terms of facts about individuals. The intellectual heritage here runs back through philosopher Karl Popper and economist Friedrich Hayek to the classical market economists and ultimately to Adam Smith. Thus, according to Popper, all social phenomena, and particularly how social institutions function, should always be understood as the result of decisions, actions, and attitudes of human individuals. We should never be satisfied with explanations presented in terms of "collectives."

According to anthropologist Tim O'Meara (1997), who has attacked the supraindividual holist position in the pages of *Current Anthropology*, the failure to achieve a scientific understanding of "human affairs" is due in large measure to the belief that there are supraindividual entities and forces. O'Meara denies the existence and causal efficacy of entities such as societies, cultures, institutions, and cultural traits—entities that he believes have no physical substance and that, in fact, do not exist in any physical sense. O'Meara insists that in "human affairs," only individual human beings exist; all else is metaphysical hocus pocus, objects and events of "weird and perplexing ontology." Thus, O'Meara writes of the "extraordinary vagueness concerning how superorganic entities exercise their peculiar influence, how individual action and supraphysical structures are linked and mediated, and how they generate, make up, or shape each other" (1997:404).

METAPHYSICAL HOCUS POCUS

As I shall show in a moment, the identification and analysis of empirical (physical) but abstract superorganic entities is a necessary and fundamental component of sociocultural science. Contra O'Meara, we have no need to abandon the 250-year-old struggle for a science of sociocultural systems and processes because of the abstract and constructed nature of these entities. But first, let me clarify my position regarding the metaphysical components in methodological holism.

At the core of methodological holism, there are three propositions:

- The whole is more than the sum of its parts and cannot be reduced to them.
- The whole determines the nature of its parts.
- The parts cannot be understood if considered in isolation from the whole.

In my view, any priority given to the whole over its parts founders on the question of how the whole is to be discerned and described. As a consequence of natural selection, humans experience the world in terms of discrete macrophysical entities such as a chair, a tree, or a person; anyone can see these things as wholes, but no one has ever seen an institution, a society, a culture, or a sociocultural system as a whole. Sociocultural wholes are necessarily knowable only through a process of logical and empirical abstraction from the observation of their parts, the smallest of which are the activities and thoughts of individuals (Harris 1964). It is illogical to assert that the whole of society and culture is more than the sum of its parts, because the only way we can get to know sociocultural wholes (as distinct from trees, chairs, or individuals) is to identify parts and the relationships among parts. You cannot see the whole of a sociocultural system the way you can see a person or a tree.

On the other hand, turning to the second point, the proposition that the whole sociocultural system determines the nature of its parts would be quite acceptable if it were accompanied by an equal emphasis upon the determination of the whole by the parts. For if we mean by *determination* some causal process such as evolution, then it is clear that selection operates on both the whole system and its parts. In other words, the whole and the parts determine each other.

Similarly, the proposition that the parts cannot be understood if considered in isolation from the whole is again reasonable, but capriciously incomplete. For we must add that the whole also cannot be understood in isolation from its parts. This emphasis upon mutual interdependence and determination, however, is better seen as the hallmark of functionalist, rather than of methodological (or metaphysical), holism (as we shall see in chapter 10).

PHYSICAL REALITY

O'Meara's rejection of sociocultural entities is based on the claim that they lack "physical reality." I am singled out as one of the anthropologists "who assert the 'reality' and 'power' of supra individualist holistic patterns that they readily acknowledge lack physical reality" (1997:400). I cannot recall ever having maintained that cultural things lack physical reality. What I have maintained is that sociocultural entities are constructed from the direct or indirect observation of the behavior and thought of specific individuals:

> Culture is a series of abstractions developed through the
> logico-empirical manipulation of data collected from the
> study of specific historic individual men and women. . . .
> (Harris 1964:172)

Apparently O'Meara equates abstractions with a lack of physical reality; but even though some cultural things cannot be touched or seen, they are nonetheless real.

The basic premise of empirical science is that there are things outside of the observer whose nature can be known only by interacting with them through observation, logical manipulation, and experiment. Thus, all things in their knowable state are *partially* the creations of observational and logical operations. This includes subatomic particles, biological species, ecosystems, tectonic plates, and weather patterns, as well as Trobriand avunculocality, Ndembu circumcision rites, General Motors, or the Soviet infrastructure.

All of the indicated sociocultural entities have a physical existence based on the direct or indirect observation of the thoughts and behavior of individual men, women, and children. True, as a result of our evolutionary careers, humans, like other animals, are equipped with certain senses that enable us to touch, see, hear, or smell some entities more immediately and more directly than others. We have a difficult time when it comes to perceiving (sensing)subatomic particles, or the molecular structure of DNA. But like most animals, humans have relatively little trouble in perceiving individual organisms, their body parts, and the environmental effects of the motions of body parts (including the sounds of speech). These body-part motions and environmental effects constitute the bedrock data upon which supraindividual but physically real sociocultural entities are (or can be) reared. As long as the model is constructed on an identifiable physical base and is built up according to explicit logical and empirical steps, it can lay claim to having a physical reality.

Some time ago, I attempted to provide a rough outline of a hierarchical series of concepts that would resolve this issue in at least a provisional and illustrative fashion. At the bottom of the hierarchy, I identified a unit called an "episode," which specified a class of body motions, environmental effects, the kinds of people involved, and where they are located in time and space (more or less who, what, when, and where). Episodes (such as a consumer tossing waste into a garbage can) form episode chains (linked to the emptying of the can by garbage collectors); episode chains form scenes (transporting waste to landfills); and scenes form serials (various activities involved in management of the landfill). All of these activities are directly observable (etically and behaviorally) and social scientists routinely identify and compare and contrast them cross-culturally (as in reportage concerning weddings, funerals, puberty rites, planting and harvesting crops, raids against enemy villages, cock fights, etc.). They possess a physical reality as surely as rocks or trees possess a physical reality.

A parallel series of models leads from individuals to groups. These form a hierarchy of progressively more inclusive and more abstract entities, starting with what I labeled nomoclones (e.g., county garbage collectors) and working up to permaclonic and superpermaclonic systems (e.g., the county waste management authority and the national system for environmental protection). Looming beyond, there are larger systems and subsystems—classes, political parties, and infrastructural, structural, and ideological formations—whose conjunction defines the total society and its culture(s). These groups and institutions, despite their abstract nature, interact with each other in ways that cannot be predicted or understood simply by the observation of the individuals and activities which are their bedrock components. Consider, for example, the interaction between General Motors and the Environmental Protection Agency. One regulates the other; the other resists. One insists on recalls for defective products; the other hires lawyers to prevent or minimize recalls. These events are based on the behavior of individuals, but in highly synoptic and abstract frames. It is true that bureaus, agencies, and departments consist of individuals behaving (and thinking) in certain ways and that we must never lose sight of this fact. At the same time, however, we must recognize that a full account of complex sociocultural systems and structures rendered in a strictly individualist perspective would be intolerably time- and labor-consuming.

Foundations of Supraindividual Holism

The perdurance of sociocultural entities invites social scientists to refer to and think in terms of institutions and organizations, traits and patterns, classes, castes, infrastructure and superstructure, and myriads of other supraindividual entities large and small. Empirical observations reveal that these entities survive the constant flux of individual native participants. Just as languages survive the death of their speakers, lineages survive the substitution of one chieftain for another, baseball teams survive the substitution of one pitcher for another, and automobile companies survive the substitution of one CEO for another.

Another reason for accepting superorganic entities is that the participants themselves carry with them emic models of the institutions, organizations, and behavioral patterns that define their social lives. While emic accounts of sociocultural systems and subsystems invite comparison with etic accounts, the participant's sense that something is out there besides individuals also needs to be respected. We are well-advised not to tell striking auto workers that there is no such thing as General Motors.

A third argument in favor of methodological holism is simply that the supraindividual models work. Whatever the ontological status of supraindividual entities, researchers who proceed on the assumption that such entities exist have been able to construct a rich body of testable theories concerning how such entities influence each other, get selected for or selected against, and thereby account for the divergent and convergent trajectories of sociocultural evolution.

HOLISM AND INDIVIDUALISM NEED EACH OTHER

Neither the methodological holists nor the methodological individualist positions can stand alone. Contrary to the holist model, culture can be seen as the creative product of individuals whose thoughts and behavior are in constant flux. This eliminates the charge that the concept of culture commits anthropology to an essentialist ontology of rigid unchanging entities that obscure the diversity and fullness of human social life. On the other hand, the holist model allows for the supraindividual nature of its higher order abstractions—as real entities that perdure across generations and that determine to a large extent what people do and think.

∼

So what is the ontological relationship between culture and the individual? It seems to me that the answer lies in accepting and combining both viewpoints, working up from the individual to the higher-order abstractions and then back down to the individual again.

With this basic feedback circuitry in place, we can turn to another fundamental quandary of science-oriented anthropology—the ethical-moral and political commitments of anthropologists and the effect these commitments have upon the viability of anthropological theories.

Chapter 4

Science, Objectivity, Morality

Under the influence of postmodernist trends (see chapter 12), anthropologists have become increasingly preoccupied with the epistemological and moral-ethical impediments against the achievement of objectivity in their cultural accounts. Many anthropologists have abandoned what Roy D'Andrade (1995:399) has called an "objective model" and have adopted a "moral model" in its place. The objective model tells about the thing being described and is conducive to testing and replication by other observers, i.e., it is science-oriented. The moral model, on the other hand, is subjective; it tells how the agent who is doing the description reacts to the object described and is aimed at identifying what is good and what is bad, rather than at what is true or false.

I share D'Andrade's general commitment to science-oriented anthropology, but cannot endorse some aspects of his argument. Specifically, I find that his treatment of the key dichotomies of objective versus subjective and science versus morality to be misleading.

PUTTING THE OBSERVER IN THE PICTURE

As I proposed in chapter 2, the difference between objective and subjective lies in the methods used to describe the phenomena under investigation—methods that are, in the one case, public, replicable, and testable and, in the other case, private, idiosyncratic, and untestable. In my view, the current postmodern preoccupation with the observer's thoughts and feelings is subjective because it involves private, idiosyncratic, and untestable operations, not because it provides information about the observer's reaction to the observed.

This again is not an inconsequential quibble. Science-oriented, objective descriptions of cultures are not impaired by an examination of the observers' reactions and biases. On the contrary, objectivity demands some account of the relationship between the describing observer and the phenomena described in order to satisfy the rule that observers specify what they have done to gain the knowledge they claim to possess. Postmodernists have a valid point when they complain that scientific descriptions conventionally remove all traces of the observer's personality in order to create what may very well be an illusory facade of objectivity. Science-oriented anthropologists need to put the observer in the picture. What we must resist are subjective accounts, as defined above, no matter whether they are about the observer or the observed.

In scientific ethnography, putting the observer in the picture requires that we know such items as where and when and why the observer was in the field, who the informants were, what language was used, and what events—such as a personal illness, emotional stress, or the actions of hostile authorities—took place that might have affected the research. In D'Andrade's approach, this kind of information would be subjective because it tells how the agent who is doing the describing reacted to the entities that are being described.

THE UNITY OF SCIENCE AND MORALITY

I turn to a second point of disagreement: D'Andrade's dichotomy between moral-subjective and scientific-objective models. D'Andrade denies that "one can blend together objectivity and morality in a single model"(1995:405). In my view, this categorical distinction needlessly concedes the moral high ground to the science-bashing camp. I agree that

scientific inquiry must be carried out in a manner that protects its findings from political-moral bias to the greatest possible degree, but this does
not mean that scientific inquiry should be (or can be) conducted in a
political-moral vacuum.

First of all there is strong empirical support for the position that
morality, in the form of culturally constructed values and preferences,
influences the definition and selection of researchable projects. What we
choose to study or not to study in the name of anthropology is a political-
moral decision. The reason for this is that we are given limited research
funding. Therefore, the allocation of research effort is a zero-sum game in
which the commitment to one kind of study means the neglect of alternative projects and agendas. The recent commitment to the study of gender
roles and ethnicity to the neglect of class stratification is an example of
political-moral choice. As another example, when structural-functional-
ism held sway, many anthropological Africanists made the political-moral
choice to ignore conflict, labor exploitation, and the whole imperialist
colonial context. This did not necessarily lessen the objectivity of their
analysis of corporate lineages or puberty ceremonies, but it certainly helped
to tarnish the reputation of anthropology as a source of political-moral
change. Similarly, as we shall see in the chapters devoted to biology and
culture, the decision to study or not to study racial and ethnic differences
has had profound political-moral consequences throughout the twentieth century.

I can illustrate the need to make a difficult political-moral choice
concerning what to study and write about from my own experience in
Portuguese Africa. As explained in its preface, I had written a pamphlet,
Portugal's African Wards,

> in order to discharge what I conceive to be a moral
> obligation. From June 1956 to May 1957 I was in
> Mozambique carrying out a research program ... In the
> course of my work I came to depend on a number of
> people, both Portuguese and Africans, for information

and assistance. To these people I became more than a
social anthropologist and even more than a friend. Many
of them risked their jobs and their personal safety to tell
me about the conditions under which they were forced to
live, even though in their own minds they could never be
entirely certain that I had not been sent to spy on them. . . .
They knew that if I wanted to, I could at least "tell the
world." Under these circumstances I cannot confine my
writings to such "neutral" or purely technical subjects as
would lead to no involvement in politically controversial
issues.

Despite this openly moral-ethical commitment, I argued that my
findings about the colonial system (the *Indigenato*) were objective, and
hence scientific. One of the main points supporting the objectivity of my
account was that my preconceptions weighed against the belief that the
Portuguese colonial system was as oppressive as it turned out to be. Since
I expected to find race relations that contrasted markedly with those of
the Union of South Africa, I could not be accused of finding in Mozambique
only what I wanted to find.

THE IMPORTANCE OF GETTING IT RIGHT

Morality blends with science in another very important way. Political-moral
decisions need to be based on the best available knowledge of what the
world is like. Science-bashers condemn science as an obstacle to the making of morally correct political decisions, but the shoe is on the other foot.
It is a lack of scientific knowledge that places our political-moral decisions
in greatest jeopardy. To claim the moral high ground, one must have reliable knowledge. We have to know what the world is like, who is doing or
has done what to whom, and who and what are responsible for the suffering and injustice we condemn and seek to remedy. If this be so, then sci-

ence-minded anthropologists may plausibly claim that their stance is not only moral, but morally superior to those who reject science as a source of reliable knowledge about the human condition. Fantasies, intuitions, interpretations, and reflections may make for good poems and novels, but if you want to know what to do about the AIDS time bomb in Africa, or landlessness in Chiapas, neglect of objective data is reprehensible.

Let me underscore the point that the blended model applies only to the extent that the blending takes place without violating the distinctive rules of scientific-objective inquiry. Distorting the data-gathering process in order to make the findings concur with a desired political-moral outcome must be vigilantly excluded. It is in this sense and only in this sense that the call for the rigid separation of the moral and science models is an ineluctable imperative.

Of course, merely following the rules of scientific inquiry does not guarantee the achievement of reliable knowledge. Scientists make mistakes, and some even cook their data; but given its many successes (in anthropology as well as in the harder sciences), science is the best-available system for providing a factual foundation for political-moral decision-making (Reyna 1993). Antiscience paradigms—such as ethnopoetics, interpretationism, hermeneutics, and phenomenology—provide no such foundation and therefore cannot be regarded as morally superior to neopositivist paradigms.

CRITICAL ANTHROPOLOGY

Disturbed by what they conceive to be anthropology's continuing support of colonial and neocolonial policies and other repressive and exploitative relationships, many anthropologists have turned toward the support and practice of what they call "critical anthropology" (Marcus and Fischer 1986). Critical anthropologists aim to expose injustice and exploitation as a new departure that supplants the false pretensions of politically free or neutral positivist approaches. A politically engaged anthropology is no novelty, however. It has roots that go back at least as far as E. B. Tylor and his identification of anthropology as "essentially a reformer's science . . . active at once in aiding progress and in removing hindrance" (quoted in Lowie 1937:83).

As will be discussed in the next several chapters, throughout the entire course of the twentieth century, a battle has raged over the relative contributions of nature and nurture to the evolution of sociocultural systems. If we take this battle into consideration, anthropology has never ceased to be "a reformer's science," or, in postmodern times, what is being called critical anthropology. It is true that much of the political thrust of anthropology in the nineteenth and early twentieth centuries was colonialist, racist, and sexist, but not liking a particular political formula does not diminish its criticality. Moreover, science-oriented anthropologists have scarcely all been hereditarians and raciologists. On the contrary, science-oriented anthropologists have a long history of contributing to the struggle against racism, antisemitism, colonialism, and sexism. Like it or not, they contributed to military and civilian intelligence gathering during World War II, and to the anti–Vietnam War movement (especially through the invention and spread of the teach-in). And all this before the current generation of critical anthropologist had gotten out of graduate school.

There is thus nothing very new, let alone startling, when critical anthropologist Nancy Scheper-Hughes writes that "if we cannot begin to think about social institutions and practices in moral or ethical terms, then anthropology strikes me as quite weak and useless" (1995:410). I agree, but only if one adds the proviso that if we cannot begin to think about social institutions and practices in scientific-objective terms then anthropology will be even weaker and more useless.

Getting It Wrong

Scheper-Hughes is justly famous for her commitment to the well-being of the people she has studied (in Ireland, Brazil, and South Africa) and for her unflinching determination to foreground the crippling effects of pov-

erty and inequality. But I see no necessary contradiction between her in-
dignation at the "medicalization" of hunger in Brazil (where she contends
the effects of hunger and chronic malnutrition are treated with tranquil-
izer pills) and the requirements of D'Andrade's objective model. Schepper-
Hughes herself almost reaches the same conclusion when she states:

> those who question the truth claims of objectivist science
> do not deny that there are discoverable "facts" in the
> world. . . . Some things are incontestably "factual" and
> these need to be studied empirically. If one is concerned
> with the number of infant deaths in rural Brazil for
> example, or the incidence of necklacing in South Africa . . .
> the researcher has a strong scientific and a moral
> imperative to get it right. (1995:436)

But she is quick to qualify this imperative with a disclaimer:

> Crucial empirical work of this kind . . . need not entail a
> philosophical commitment to Enlightenment notions of
> reason and truth. (1995:436)

Instead of being guided by such notions, which lead one to positivism and
false certainties, the new brand of empirical studies

> can be guided by critical-interpretive concerns about the
> inevitable partiality of truth and about the various
> meanings that "facts" and "events" have in the existential,
> cultural, and political sense. (1995:436)

These ruminations do not add up to a coherent set of principles
adequate for guiding the conduct of politically responsible research. If there
are some things that we need to get right, then there must be other things
that we don't need to worry about getting wrong. But just what are the
things we need to get right and what are the things we can get wrong?

Without a coherent set of methodological principles for distinguishing between research that requires empirical data and research that is free of such a requirement, we would obviously be better off sticking to the maligned "Enlightenment notions of reason and truth," since we have no way of knowing that the "inevitable partiality" will be less partial for the critical anthropologist than for those who follow different approaches. Merely telling us that facts and events have different meanings is of little use. Why should we attend to some meanings and not to others?

$\sim$

Unlike postmodernists, whom she felicitously excoriates for their relativism and obscurantism (more about this in chapter 12), Scheper-Hughes intends to "speak truth to power." This is a noble ambition, but I cannot see how she expects to do this and at the same time accept the Foucauldian mantra that "the objectivity of science and of medicine is always a phantom objectivity." I would argue to the contrary: without science, morality is always a phantom morality. Without science, critical anthropology will dissolve back into the postmodernist mainstream, where radical skepticism, relativism, and nihilism are the order of the day (Gross and Levitt 1994; Rosenau 1992).

There is more than a little irony in the critical stance Scheper-Hughes and other critical theorists take toward the Enlightenment. For activists interested in defying the powerful and defending the poor and the weak, what better source of inspiration for these views can be found than the works of Rousseau, Condorcet, and Thomas Paine? As recounted in chapter 6 to come, prominent conservative voices, such as the authors of the notorious *The Bell Curve* (Herrnstein and Murray 1995), join Scheper-Hughes in decrying the influence of the Enlightenment precisely because, for conservatives, the Enlightenment is the main source of noxious wrong-headed ideas about equality.

Part II

Biology and Culture

Chapter 5

De-Biologizing Culture: The Boasians

As I remarked a few pages back, throughout the entire course of the twentieth century, proponents of biological and cultural theories of the evolution of sociocultural systems have battled each other. On one side are the biologizers—those who invoke a suite of hereditarian, racial, and genetic factors in explaining cultural differences and similarities; and on the other side are the de-biologizers—those who stress learning and the influence of the environment.

By mid-century, the learning-environmentalists seemed to have gained the upper hand. More recently however, the biologizers have regained much of the support they enjoyed early in the century.

RACIOLOGY, EUGENICS, AND HEREDITARIANISM

At the beginning of the twentieth century, established scientific authorities and the public saw the human species as divided into a small number of permanent and ancient races that possessed distinctive cultures and spoke related languages. These races, languages and cultures were ranked into superior and inferior types, as judged by the primarily white and Euro-

This chapter is based in part on a paper presented September 16, 1996, at the New York Academy of Sciences. The lecture was sponsored by the Columbia University Department of Anthropology and the Columbia Graduate Anthropology Alumni Association in celebration of a century of anthropology in New York City.

American academic establishment. The vast majority of scholars attributed this hierarchical order to the outcome of Herbert Spencer's and Charles Darwin's "struggle for survival" (a phrase that originated with Spencer and was taken over by Darwin).

For Spencer and other social Darwinists (or biological Spencerists, as I would prefer), eliminating "inferior" individuals and races with their "inferior" languages and cultures was a natural and inevitable outcome of competition. Superior races would soon replace inferior ones if the evolutionary process was allowed to take its course. Subsequently, the English scientist Francis Galton (1908) made the disturbing (to him) discovery that the "inferior races" were actually outbreeding the supposedly superior ones. This discovery gave rise to the eugenics movement. As we shall see in chapter 8, the fecundity of disadvantaged social strata continues to confound modern neo-Darwinists, who emphasize "reproductive success" as the sole measure of evolutionary fitness.

The eugenicists argued that Nature could not be allowed to take its course any longer. Inferior but fertile human specimens from Asia and from southern and eastern Europe had to be prevented from entering the United States and other advanced societies; or if they succeeded in gaining entry, they had to be prevented from reproducing. According to Charles Davenport (1912:219), mass compulsory sterilization was the only way to deal with those who possessed "imbecile, epileptic, insane, criminalistic" germ plasm. Into the 1920s, the views of eugenicists like Galton, Davenport, and Harvard professor Roland Dixon (1923) still prevailed at the highest levels of academia and government. In signing the 1924 immigration law, President Calvin Coolidge declared:

America must be kept American. Biological laws show that Nordics deteriorate when mixed with other races. (Quoted in Stoskopf 1996)

In a horrific sense, Hitler's "final solution" represented a speeded-up version of eugenics—the one seeking "racial purity" through prolonged control over breeding; the other through immediate mass murder.

In the "nature versus nurture" debate—a pithy phrase which we also owe to Galton—the eugenicists were necessarily devoted hereditarians. It was their denial that the human condition could be significantly altered by manipulating the environment that provided the rationale for sterilization and other forms of eugenic intervention.

OPPOSITION TO BIOLOGIZED THEORIES OF CULTURE

Franz Boas and his students did much to challenge, if not disprove, the prevailing belief that race, language, and culture were inseparable and that some races, languages, and cultures were better, more civilized, and more fit to survive than others. Boas stated in his book, *The Mind of Primitive Man* (1911:278),

> I hope the discussions outlined in these pages have shown
> that the data of anthropology teach us a greater tolerance
> of forms of civilization different from our own, that we
> should learn to look on foreign races with greater
> sympathy and with a conviction that, as all races in the
> past have contributed to cultural progress in one way or
> another, so they will be capable of advancing the interests
> of mankind if we are only willing to give them a fair
> opportunity.

With the appointment of Boas as lecturer in physical anthropology in 1896 (Lesser 1981) the Department of Anthropology at Columbia University became a world center of scholarly opposition to the regnant biologized and raciological theories of culture. At the core of the Boasian attempt to refute the hereditarian adversaries was the first-hand empirical knowledge of radically non-Western tribal, band, and village forms of cultures. Boas and his students gained this knowledge through empirical field research, primarily among North American Indians. To correct the conflation of race, language, and culture, they showed that tribes or bands or villages possessing similar cultures often spoke dissimilar and mutually unintelligible languages. They also showed that although some Native Americans seemed to be racially similar, their cultures could be remarkably different. Moreover, upon close inspection, Native American's languages and cultures turned out to be anything but proof of racial inferiority. Their complex kinship systems, their rich religious and ritual life, and their ingenious and efficient technologies weighed against raciological and hereditarian doctrines. So did the discovery that the languages spoken by supposedly "primitive" peoples possessed complex and nuanced grammars that were capable of expressing the most subtle and exalted thoughts. In the words of Boasian linguist Edward Sapir (1921:234),

> When it comes to linguistic form, Plato walks with the Macedonian swineherd, Confucius with the headhunting savages of Assam.

Margaret Mead, Boas's most famous student, directly attacked the hereditarian position in her book *Coming of Age in Samoa* (1928). She attempted to show that biological factors in adolescence were less powerful as determinants of behavior than were cultural factors. Derek Freeman's (1983) critique notwithstanding, Mead effectively challenged the then-overwhelmingly dominant hereditarian viewpoint. Although Mead may have inadvertently misrepresented some aspects of adolescent behavior among the Samoans, the existence of culturally constructed variations in the degree of adolescent sexual freedom is well-established (Schlegel and Barry 1991). On the other hand, as Paul Shankman (1996) maintains, Freeman's account may be as factually deficient as Mead's and the issue is far from decided.

Despite the continuing popularity of the old raciological and hereditarian principles in the 1910s, Boas and his students were able to gain a strong foothold in academia. They were aided by a shift in the provenance of America's immigrant tide from northwestern to southern and eastern Europe. By World War I, this influx led to the formation of new political constituencies that contested WASP hegemony and were more receptive to Boasian principles.

Nonetheless, Boasian anthropology did not achieve dominance prior to the late 1930s. During the 1920s, anthropologists at Harvard such as Aleš Hrdlička and Ernest Hooton remained staunch advocates of Nordic superiority, eugenics, and the exclusion of immigrants from Asia and southern and eastern Europe. At this time, the major prestigious private universities, including Columbia, still openly expressed their opposition to admitting Jews and other "inferior races" (Sacks 1994). The muting of racist, raciological, and hereditarian voices cannot be attributed to new discoveries damaging to the raciological and hereditarian positions. What tipped the balance toward the Boasians were the events that were sweeping the world toward the catastrophe of World War II. With capitalism in crisis, racist and hereditarian theories achieved new prominence in American and European politics.

In Germany, the Nazis were making racial purity and Teutonic supremacy central themes of their push for power, while in the United States, millions listened to the weekly racist ranting of Father Coughlin's radio addresses. Anti-Semitism was widely preached and practiced among both scientists and working-class elements, who needed scapegoats on which to blame their economic and social crises. It would be entirely inappropriate for me to list the names of Boasians who, in addition to Boas himself, acknowledged descent from Jewish parents; and in no way would I wish to promote the idea that the mobilization of anthropological knowledge in the struggle against anti-Semitism in the 1930s solely depended on the initiative of people of Jewish descent. It cannot be denied, however, that the prospect of being a prime target of fulminating "race" hatred strongly concentrates one's mind on refuting racist, raciological, and hereditarian points of view.

Coincident with the outbreak of World War II, the credibility of racist, raciological, and hereditarian viewpoints decreased. With the Germans calling themselves the "master race" and vowing to rule over Europe for a thousand years, open advocacy of racist, raciological, and hereditarian theories fell into disrepute. Since the allies depicted World War II as "the war to make the world safe for democracy," espousals of racist and hereditarian theories were officially regarded as seditious impediments to the prosecution of the war effort. The Nazi's crackpot theories of Teutonic supremacy gave rise to repugnance and fear as the allies became more familiar with the existence of death camps and crematoria dedicated to the extermination of Jews, Gypsies, and homosexuals.

With their viewpoints receiving official backing, Boasians such as Ruth Benedict (1940; 1943), Gene Weltfish (Benedict and Weltfish 1947), Margaret Mead (1942) and many others (including Boas himself up to his death in 1942), produced an outpouring of books, magazine articles, and pamphlets for mass consumption that aimed at combating racist and hereditarian doctrines. (Let me note parenthetically that, during World War II, anthropologists were not merely recruited or encouraged to write in support of the war effort, but to a surprising degree were involved in clandestine operations on behalf of the predecessor of the CIA and other government intelligence agencies about which little has been known [Price 1996].)

While the Boasian viewpoint made considerable headway as a result of its contribution to the war effort, powerful racist and hereditarian countercurrents persisted. The American military, for example, remained segregated by race and sex to the war's end, not to mention the persistent portrayal of the Japanese enemy as a race apart, without redeeming features.

Nonetheless, World War II tipped the academic balance in favor of Boasian principles. During the 1950s and 1960s, anthropologists trained by Boas provided many of the scientific and political-ideological arguments taken up by the civil rights movement and affirmative action. It was at this time also that Boas's critique of raciology, as synthesized by Columbia-trained Ashley Montagu, provided the basis for UNESCO's "Statement by Experts On Race Problems" (1950).

World War II created an ambience favorable to the Boasians in another respect. It provided returning veterans (of which there were some fourteen million) with access to university degrees, previously inaccessible to members of the lower-middle and working classes and the ethnic minorities. The Columbia department, in particular, owed much of its scholarly and political activism on behalf of Boasian antihereditarian and antiracist principles to the influx of these left-leaning students and instructors.

During the 1970s and 1980s, a popular backlash developed among working- and middle-class whites against the welfare state, the war on poverty, affirmative action, and other "nurture" programs of the Great Society. We see now, in retrospect, that many anthropologists were lulled into a false sense of security by the seeming triumph of the Boasian position on race and heredity, and that they miscalculated the strength of the reaction that was forming. Indeed, during the seventies and eighties, studies of race became unfashionable, the topic disappeared from many textbooks, and many anthropologists refused to discuss the subject because they believed that race was not a biologically valid taxonomic category for describing human populations. If race had any reality, it was as "social race"—an emic, culturally constructed concept on the level of a folk tale (Paredes 1997).

Some scholars, including members of an official committee of the American Anthropological Association (*Anthropology Newsletter*, April 1997:1), suggested that anthropologists stop using the word race altogether. In 1985, only 50 percent of physical anthropologists and 30 percent of cultural anthropologists at degree-granting departments agreed with the statement that "there are biological races in the species *H. sapiens*"(Lieberman and Kirk 1996), and only a handful of introductory textbooks covered the subject (Shanklin 1994). Yet the term cannot be totally useless in biological discourse, for why else would Charles Darwin have put it on the title page of

> *The Origin of Species: By Means Of Natural Selection Or*
> *The Preservation Of Favored Races In The Struggle For Life?*

CONFRONTING THE EMICS OF RACE

The proposal to expunge the word *race* from scholarly discourse as a means of combating racism and raciological perspectives can only increase the already widespread suspicion that anthropologists are an eccentric tribe.

To assert that human races do not exist is certain to bewilder people whose entire lives have been twisted and shaped by their experiences as members of one race or another. Clearly the existence of human races in an emic sense cannot be a matter of controversy.

Much of the confusion surrounding the definition of race arises from the not unusual fact that the emic and etic versions do not match. Indeed, not only don't they match, but they are in direct opposition to each other at numerous points. Given the great political-moral importance of the race concept, it remains a prime obligation of anthropology to confront the emic versions of race and to subject them to rigorous scrutiny in order to expose the fallacies they embody. There is much more to be gained from exposing these fallacies—from saying what is wrong with popular notions about race—than there is to be gained from trying to define race in positive etic terms agreeable to all observers. I won't attempt to supply an exhaustive list of all the errors and misconceptions embodied in popular definitions of race. The more fallacies that are presented, the more likely that we shall encounter dissenting opinions concerning their etic status. There are, however, certain key points to which most anthropologists subscribe and that can safely be juxtaposed against the emic fallacies.

For example, high on any list of basic fallacies embraced by the emics of race is the belief that there is a fixed and scientifically agreed-upon number of human races. On the contrary, at least fourteen different race typologies have been used or proposed by physical anthropologists during the twentieth century (Molnar 1983:19), some with only four or five races such as Australoids, Capoids, Caucasoids, Congoids, and Mongoloids (Coon 1965); others with as many as thirty-two (Molnar 1992:25). Some physical anthropologists distinguished racial "stocks," which they divided into thirty different races, splitting Caucasians into Baltics, Nordics, Alpines, Dinarics, and Mediterraneans. The large number of different etic typologies results from the use of different classificatory criteria by different investigators: some emphasize blood groups; others concentrate on skin color, cranial and skeletal features; others focus on DNA. Since all these features occur discordantly (don't stay together as a package), the resulting typologies can be viewed as arbitrary demarcations that lack biological significance (as compared, for example, with the biological significance of organisms that belong to different species).

Another common fallacy is the belief that human races can't or don't normally interbreed. On the contrary, all known human populations can mate and have fertile offspring regardless of their etic race. Moreover, at every geographical or social boundary between major populations, one finds evidence of gene flow in the form of intermediate gene frequencies. For thousands of years, military conquests have resulted in new genetic patterns indicative of widespread interbreeding. In more recent times, huge migrations (voluntary and forced) have resulted in new patterns of genetic diversity throughout the Western Hemisphere and in much of Africa. In addition, as a consequence of industrial globalization, we can expect these new races to become even more common and to spread further over broader regions and prevail against any isolating tendencies.

Yet another fallacy is the popular belief that an individual's emic racial identity is determined by biological ancestry. In fact, in the United States and other race-conscious societies, racial identity is assigned to individuals according to arbitrary rules of descent instead of according to biological criteria. In the United States, the "one drop of blood" rule still prevails. Having a single ancestor of a particular emic race is sufficient to establish one's racial identity. Thus, if one parent is black and the other white, all of their children are blacks. But the biological fact is that we inherit half of our cell-nucleus genes from father and half from mother.

Finally, there is the fallacy that would have us believe that races have their own languages and cultures. This, of course returns us to the mother error of racism and raciology, which Boas and his students thought had been laid to rest. It is obvious that, among races that occupy continents or subcontinents, there is at least as much cultural and linguistic variation within them as between them. A race is not a culture. Race is people; culture is a way of life. Each major continental race does not have just one culture; each has hundreds of different cultures. And these cultures cover the whole spectrum of cultural types, from bands and villages to states and empires. Thus people who belong to different biological races may possess very similar, or even identical cultures. In the United States, millions of racially diverse children and grandchildren of Asians and Africans have a way of life that is essentially similar to the way of life of the "Caucasian" majority. These biological and anthropological facts, however, are often ignored in the construction of social races. This is an issue I shall discuss further in chapter 9 with regard especially to the concept of "African culture."

RACE AND DISEASE

As noted previously, many beliefs about race are caught up in continuing controversies that await resolution through more research. I have in mind especially the recognition by medical researchers that the genes for certain diseases occur with higher frequency in some populations than in others. In deciding on the diagnosis and treatment for such diseases, it is sometimes important to know whether the patient is a member of the susceptible group. Tay-Sachs disease, for example, which destroys the central nervous system, is controlled by a gene that is relatively common among Jews descended from East Europeans. Genes for sickle-cell anemia are relatively common among West Africans. Blacks in the United States also are at higher risk for high blood pressure and diabetes.

Does this not show the importance and biological integrity of racial classification? Yes and no. First of all, the Tay-Sachs gene is extremely rare—only one in six thousand births is affected, so this gene can scarcely serve as a marker of racial identity. The sickle-cell gene, on the other hand, occurs quite frequently among West African blacks but hardly at all in many other parts of Africa (its distribution is related to the distribution of malaria). Therefore, one can scarcely define an African race on the basis of the gene for sickling. As for hypertension and diabetes, the implications are quite different. The genes for these diseases have not been identified; and since blacks in Africa rarely suffer from either of these conditions, it is likely that their occurrence reflects environmental rather than genetic influences. In any event, harm may result from too great a dependence on racial hypotheses to the neglect of sociocultural and other environmental stresses.

~

In retrospect, we see that the raciological, hereditarian, and other biologized approaches to the explanation of sociocultural differences and similarities had merely been muted or driven underground. Their allure as a means of justifying and explaining income and wealth disparities, the growth of an underclass, crime, and other social pathologies assured their return. Today, welfare capitalism and its nurturance programs are in full retreat before a rising tide of biologized, raciological, and hereditarian theories and practices. In the next several chapters, we will look more closely at some of the specific arenas in which the resurgence of biologized theories of culture is taking place.

Chapter 6

Biologizing Inequality

The struggle over the significance of racial IQ scores is more than just a matter of whose science is to be believed; it also has always involved a clash between different visions of the good society, especially with respect to the problem of inequality. With eugenic solutions politically unacceptable, IQ's true believers are left with the difficult task of teaching people how to feel comfortable living in a society that is divided and unequal and that supposedly will always be divided and unequal.

In 1994, Harvard psychologist Richard Herrnstein and political scientist Charles Murray published *The Bell Curve*, a book that not only argues for the unmodifiability of IQ but that advocates a permanent class structure involving inequalities based on intelligence. In this chapter I concentrate on spelling out just what kind of class structure and political program Herrnstein and Murray have in mind for America in the new millenium. I shall leave it to the reader to decide whether the political ramifications of the Bell Curve are on the side of tragedy or comedy.

THE AMERICAN CLASS STRUCTURE ACCORDING TO HERRNSTEIN AND MURRAY

The authors tell us that they wrote *The Bell Curve*, in order to explain certain "strange things" that are happening in American society. The strange things in question center on the formation of an increasingly polarized and dysfunctional class structure. This structure currently has three components: a relatively small upper class, a large middle class, and a small lower segment. They call the upper group the "cognitive elite" in recognition of the increasingly important role that intelligence plays in becoming one of the "fortunate few." The bottom segment is the "underclass," a group that has low intelligence and that is afflicted with many sociopathic dysfunctions.

The Cognitive Elite

For people in the cognitive elite, life is getting better—they go to the best colleges, earn six-figure salaries, and do what they enjoy doing. While intelligence has always maintained some presence in ruling strata throughout history, the development of computerized, symbol-processing technologies has placed an unprecedented premium on cognitive capabilities. Never before, Herrnstein and Murray argue, have the wealthy and powerful been so intermingled and so thoroughly screened for high intelligence. Never before have the interests of the rich and powerful coincided so closely with the interests of people who have high IQs. Never has there been a time when it was so consistently and universally advantageous to be smart (Herrnstein and Murray 1994:27).

Herrnstein and Murray discern far-reaching effects emanating from the formation of this cognitive elite. They see more than the outlines of a new class structure; they see the beginnings of a meritocracy, a whole new form of society in which wealth and power are distributed according to intelligence. (Some critics suggest that "testocracy" would be a more appropriate label in view of the salience of intelligence tests in establishing Herrnstein and Murray's notions of merit.)

The Underclass

As for the people in the underclass, life is getting steadily worse. They suffer from poverty, drug addiction, incarceration for violent crimes, broken families, incompetent parenting, and welfare dependency. Unable to master the new technologies, they are being left further and further behind the rest of the population. For them, meritocracy means a confirmed ticket to the worst seat in the house.

The Cognitive Middle

Up to this point, I have been presenting Herrnstein and Murray's picture of the relatively small segments at the extremes of the class structure—the "tails" of the bell curve. However, the majority of Americans are said to occupy an intermediary position. While these middling types are smart enough to take care of themselves, they are being increasingly squeezed and pummeled "by the power of the cognitive elite and the plight of the underclass." Both the cognitive elite and the middle segment are becoming increasingly angry and resentful about the costs incurred in trying to protect themselves from criminal attacks and from the costs of various tax-based interventions and subventions. They fear for their safety and grow impatient with laws that protect the perpetrators rather than the victims. As a result, "the fragile web of civility, mutual regard, and mutual obligation" that is needed for a "happy society" is being "torn" apart.

THE RISE OF THE CUSTODIAL STATE

Herrnstein and Murray warn that if no remedy for these conditions is found, the underclass will be subject to harsh and vindictive treatment and a new and unwanted form of social formation will emerge. Herrnstein and Murray name this unhappy form of social life the "custodial state." Its major characteristics will include stricter law enforcement, aggressive sentencing, stop and frisk arrests, more prisons, and high-tech bracelets and other restraining devices. The authors also predict that the rise of the

custodial state will mean a return to pre–civil-rights-era racism. No more
Mr. Nice Guy cognitive elites. No more tiptoeing around the issue of racial
inferiority. The get-tough custodians will demand a frank accounting of
the genetic basis of the cognitive disabilities of African Americans and other
troublemakers in the underclass.

> In short, by custodial state we have in mind a high tech
> and more lavish version of the Indian Reservation for
> some substantial minority of the nation's population,
> while the rest of America tries to go about its business. In
> its less benign forms, the solution will become more and
> more totalitarian. (526)

The authors do not spell out what a more lavish version of an Indian
Reservation would be like, but the image they conjure up in my mind is
that of a camp with barbed wire. An important part of the authors' dire
prophesies is that in setting up and running the apparatus of the custodial
state, America will destroy its most hallowed traditions:

> It is difficult to imagine the United States preserving its
> heritage of individualism, equal rights before the law, and
> free people running their own lives, once it is accepted that
> a significant part of the population must be made
> permanent wards of the state. (526)

Having implanted this horrifying vision of dystopia in our heads,
the authors prepare to move on to the question of how America can be
prevented from developing into a totalitarian custodial state. You might
suppose, given the gravity of our situation, that some strong and danger-
ous medicine would be recommended at this point. But not so.

IQ Is Destiny

What we have to do is to comprehend and incorporate into the center of our consciousness the decisive role of IQ in shaping social life in general and American society in particular. According to Herrnstein and Murray, social scientists, journalists, and politicians who have previously sought to identify the source of our societal discontents have all been wide of the mark. The problem is that while we have closely examined changes in the economy, demography, and culture, we have

> ignored an underlying element that has shaped these changes: human intelligence—the way it varies within the American population and its crucially changing role in our destinies during the last half of the twentieth century. To try to come to grips with the nation's problems without understanding the role of intelligence is to see through a glass darkly indeed, to grope with symptoms instead of causes, to stumble into supposed remedies that have no chance of working. (xxiii)

Low IQ Causes Social Pathologies vs. Social Pathologies Cause Low IQ

Herrnstein and Murray are on solid ground when they show that IQ is correlated with many of the principal dysfunctions of contemporary society. Thus, the lower a group's IQ, the worse the jobs, the greater the unemployment, the greater the poverty and economic miseration, the higher the crime rate, the higher the drop out rate the greater the rate of unwed motherhood, the weaker the family, the worse the parenting, the greater the dependence on welfare.

It seems almost self-evident that, in a competitive society, individuals who have low IQs are more likely to suffer from dysfunctions than individuals who have high IQs. I hasten to add that this does not mean I accept the claim that low IQ causes these problems. Herrnstein and Murray are well aware that statistical correlations do not indicate which variable, if any, is the cause of another(567). As Murray himself states flatly in his afterword to the paperback edition:

> The nonexperimental social sciences cannot demonstrate
> unequivocal causality.

This dictum does not prevent Herrnstein and Murray from sliding into usages that imply that low IQ *is* a cause of low-paying jobs, unemployment, high crime, etc., or that IQ *is* a significant determinant of these dysfunctions.

To add more confusion, the authors present causal issues in the form of evasive questions, such as:

> Could low intelligence possibly be a cause of irresponsible
> childbearing and parenting behavior . . .? Could low
> intelligence possibly be a cause of unemployment or
> poverty? (117–8)

Phrased in this fashion how could anyone possibly say no? On the other hand, nothing prevents us from turning the indicated causal relationship upside down, for example: Could irresponsible child bearing and parenting behavior possibly be a cause of low IQ? Could unemployment and poverty possibly be a cause of low IQ? Again, who could possibly say no? But Herrnstein and Murray only take the first possibility seriously.

Let us now see how the authors propose to use knowledge of the allegedly unmodifiable and causal effects of IQ to prevent the rise of a totalitarian custodial state.

LEARNING TO LIVE WITH INEQUALITY

According to Herrnstein and Murray, once it is realized that IQ sets unalterable, genetically determined limits on the kinds of remedial programs that can be implemented on behalf of the underclass by well-meaning members of the cognitive elite, the way will be cleared to get rid of long-standing conceptual errors about the human condition. At last the cognitive elite and the cognitive middle will awaken to the fact that the underclass is simply not smart enough to function effectively in the increasingly complex and technical postmodern social milieu. A new and more realistic attitude toward inequality will emerge in which the centuries-old Enlightenment doctrine that equality can be achieved and practiced by everyone will be driven from our minds and from our institutions. (Note that this disparagement of the Enlightenment gives Scheper-Hughes and other advocates of critical anthropology some strange bedfellows.) Once everyone learns that people are not created equal in intelligence and that intelligence increasingly determines class identity, the blinders will fall from our eyes and we will be able to design a better America. In other words, Herrnstein and Murray want us to believe that our basic problems arise from having too much equality in our lives. We need to learn to live with more inequality:

> It is time for America once again to try living with inequality . . . (551)

There are two ways to interpret this exhortation. One is that we have not really been living in a society plagued by racism, sexism, and poverty where the average CEO makes over one hundred times what the average worker does, and 10 percent of the households have a net worth more than two times greater than the net worth of 90 percent of the remaining households (Kennichel 1996). The other is that we are being exhorted to return to the good old days when people of wealth and status felt no shame for not feeling responsible for advancing the welfare of the underclass.

VALUED PLACES

No doubt the realization on the part of members of the underclass that
they are irredeemably stupid will provoke some of them to protest the fate
they have been dealt by nature, but these malcontents can be steered away
from their troublesome thoughts by learning (with the help of the cognitive elite) how to reevaluate their situation. While it is nice to enjoy the
benefits of high IQ, one's sense of self-worth need not depend on intellectual achievement. Herrnstein and Murray don't actually say this, but the
unctuous tone is true to that of the original. But to continue. Invoking the
experience of past centuries, the authors reach the conclusion that what
matters in life is not income and wealth, but finding a "valued place" in
society. They explain,

> You occupy a valued place if other people would miss you
> if you were gone. (535)

This is a heavy mental burden to place upon our dumbest citizens.
How shall they know in advance of going aloft that they will be missed. Or
perhaps it doesn't matter, and all one need do to find a valued place is to
imagine you will be missed. One should also not rule out the possibility
that the cognitive elite will form a committee to hand out certificates of
valued places in the way that bosses used to bestow gold watches on their
faithful employees.

INCREASING THE NUMBER OF VALUED PLACES

Undeterred by such trivia, Herrnstein and Murray present a plan for increasing the number of valued places in a stratified postmodern society
such as ours. Their recommendations flow from a series of unwittingly
embarrassing caricatures of what Ferdinand Tonnies called *Gemeinschaft*
and Robert Redfield called "the folk community." In former times (not

precisely identified), when people lived on farms and in small towns and neighborhoods, it was much easier for those of low intellectual ability to find valued places. Just getting married and raising a family established a web of valued places in those halcyon bygone days:

> Anyone who wanted to have a valuable place could find
> one in the local school boards, churches, union halls,
> garden clubs, and benevolent associations of one sort or
> another. . . . Someone who was mentally ill or a bit dull
> might not be chosen to head up the parish clothing drive
> but was certainly eligible to help out. (537)

Our authors take pains to point out that the inventory of valued places did not depend on big government providing assistance to towns or neighborhoods. Most functions—police, charity, welfare, education— were fulfilled by local institutions. They do not deny that these communities experienced some dysfunctions:

> All sorts of human problems from wretched marriages to
> neighborhood feuds and human misery could be found
> but there was no dearth of valued places. (537)

When the responsibilities of marriage and parenthood were clear and uncompromising and when the "stuff" (their word) of community life had to be carried out by the neighborhood or it wouldn't get done, society was full of valued places for people of a broad range of abilities.

Herrnstein and Murray claim that there is one thing that everybody agrees on: during the past thirty years, American communities have been drained or stripped of this "stuff" of community life. (539) Something vital and important has been drained out of them. For large segments of America, however, the neighborhood community still offers the best prospect for reinfusing life with meaning, whether one's IQ is high or low.

POLICY RECOMMENDATIONS

At last we reach the moment of truth, when Herrnstein and Murray must explain how their proposal for learning to live with inequality can be implemented through practical policy. By my count, they make four policy proposals.

- Return social functions to the neighborhood. This will increase the number of valued places, as explained above. The beauty of this proposal is that the neighborhood's valued places will expand automatically if the government just steps back and stops meddling in local affairs. Government policy thus can do much to foster the vitality of neighborhoods by trying to do less for them.
- Reduce complexity, simplify rules, eliminate bureaucracy. There are too many forms to fill out, too many regulations, too much small print. Reducing paperwork and eliminating bureaus will reduce the power of the cognitive elite, who are the only ones who benefit from complexity.
- Make criminal justice clear and prompt. Concentrate criminal justice on a few clearly defined crimes that everybody agrees are wrong. Administer punishment that "hurts" and do it promptly upon conviction. This recommendation appears to be aimed primarily at the underclass. People of limited intelligence can be kept in line by commandments like "thou shalt not steal," not by commandments that say "thou shalt not steal, unless you have a good reason." No mention is made here of cognitive-elite white-collar crime whose consequences can be quite violent for thousands.
- Return marriage to its formerly unique legal status. Marriage and raising a family are the most prolific sources of valued places for people of low intelligence. The ability to have sex without marriage confuses such people. Marriage should once again become the sole legal method of obtaining rights over children.

These recommendations scarcely encourage a belief that allowing a larger role to IQ in the allocation of wealth and power will avoid the social, political, and environmental catastrophes that lie over the horizon. The policy recommendations for learning to live with (read accept or submit to) inequality seem impractical in the extreme, for they all depend on solidifying and even increasing the potential for conflict between the ruling elites and the other classes. Or are Herrnstein and Murray cryptorevolutionaries bent on starting a full-scale class and ethnic war? How dumb do people have to be not to see that meritocracy and valued places are ideological smokescreens behind which the political-economic elite, together with their cognitive henchmen, will carry on their usual greedy scramble for wealth and power? Or, in the words of Loring Brace,

> all would be well if the congenitally inferior could be
> brought to accept their lot and be happy hewing the wood
> and drawing the water for their cognitive betters.
> (1996:157)

As for returning to the neighborhoods of the past, not until you press the undo button and go back to preindustrial and precapitalist times. The technological and political economic forces that destroyed the "little community" of Robert Redfield or the *Gemeinschaft* of Ferdinand Tönnies—the urbanization, industrialization, commodification, and class, gender, and racial discrimination that some call capitalism—are more powerful than ever. Making provisions for the "affordable housing" of people of low intelligence is not likely to appeal to the local elites who have spent the better part of their lives trying to avoid such people in order to protect real estate values.

NEGLECTED CAUSES AND PROCESSES

Herrnstein and Murray's wacky policy proposals are consistent with their interpretation of the central features of IQ. Since IQ is essentially unmodifiable according to Herrnstein and Murray, it cannot be a vehicle for improving social life. It cannot be the lever that lifts and redistributes the social burdens we all carry. Its explanatory scope is similarly inconsequential. While IQ may be a good predictor of how social wealth and power are apportioned, it is overshadowed by many other variables that fall outside the range of the author's interests and competence.

IQ, high or low, cannot explain the presence of unemployment, unrewarding jobs, poverty, and crime. Low IQ can explain why certain kinds of people are more likely to get laid off during a downsizing than others, but it cannot tell us why the downsizing and layoffs take place. Is it because the IQ scores of the CEOs suddenly drop (or suddenly rise)?

Let me pursue the problem of employment a little further, since it is connected to so many other indices of social well-being. Herrnstein and Murray's correlations show that IQ is a better predictor of who will become unemployed than socioeconomic status. Young men with very low IQs are twice as likely to experience being out of the labor force for a month or more than young men with very high IQs (159), but this tells us nothing about why the rate of unemployment varied from as low as 3 percent in the 1950s to as high as 10 percent in the 1980s and back down to 4 percent in the 1990s.

It would be unfair to say that Herrnstein and Murray entirely ignore the fact that the processes that produce inequality and social dysfunctions are deeply embedded in the structural (political-economic) level of social phenomena. Thus, in discussing the role of IQ in relation to unemployment, they refer to "large macroeconomic forces which we will not try to cover" (157).

In view of Herrnstein and Murray's claim that IQ is the social world's prime mover—its supreme influence—I would expect them to give some estimate concerning the importance of the omitted forces. Any explanation of rates of employment would illustrate that IQ is a sideshow, not a main feature, in the struggle for America's future. One cannot understand employment and wage rates without considering the role of the Federal Reserve in setting interest rates and controlling inflation, the weakening of the labor unions through the hiring of permanent replacements during strikes, the disciplining of workers through the threat of downsizing and mergers, access to cheap labor on a global scale, replacement of workers by machines, and many other political-economic processes. It is hard to see how IQ—especially an *unchanging* IQ—can explain any part of the historical variations that surround employment and wage-rate policies. IQ can tell us who is likely to gain and who is likely to lose, who will be in the cognitive elite and who will be in the underclass; but it cannot tell us why there has to be a cognitive elite and an underclass.

~

One of Herrnstein and Murray's most persistent themes is that American social policy has operated in an unrealistic intellectual milieu. "We never quite say it in so many words," Murray informs us in his afterword, but the book's subtext is that America's discussion of social policy since the 1960s has been carried out in a never-never land, where human beings are easily changed and everyone can become above average as in Lake Wobegon. It is clear, however, that Herrnstein and Murray have their own never-never land gated community in the sky, where the great god IQ reigns and none but Harvard smarts may enter.

Chapter 7

IQ Is Not Forever

IQ AND RACE

Among the intellectual programs directly or indirectly aimed at reinstating pre-Boasian approaches to the explanation of cultural differences, IQ studies are among the most egregious. It has long been known that, nationwide, American whites score an average of fifteen points higher on various kinds of intelligence tests than do American blacks. When samples of blacks and whites are matched for socioeconomic status—income, job type, and years of schooling—a seven-point difference remains. Hereditarians like Herrnstein and Murray conclude, therefore, that there are permanent, innate, genetically determined intelligence differences between blacks and whites. Anthropology must participate in the evaluation of these dubious findings.

PROBLEMS OF RESEARCH DESIGN

First there is the question of whether IQ scores are the measure of anything other than the ability to take intelligence tests, leaving other forms of intelligence, such as aesthetic sensitivity and empathic resonance, unmeasured. Then there is the question, which can be posed in many different forms, as to whether the matching of socioeconomic variables is as close as the hereditarians avow. Anthropologists in the Boasian tradition have always stressed the difficulty of devising tests that are uninfluenced by culture, forcefully asserting that "There is no possibility of any intelligence test not being culturally biased" (Bohannon 1973:96).

The most vulnerable part of the hereditarian claim about matching blacks and whites for socioeconomic status is the inability to control for the effects on blacks of being members of a subordinated and disparaged minority. More specifically, no matching of socioeconomic criteria can cancel out the effects of what John Hoberman (1997:52) has called the "athleticizing of the Black mind." It is a legacy of slavery that the black minority's self-esteem has been built around prowess in sports rather than around a tradition that honors scholastic and intellectual achievements.

In order to control for the effect of being in a subordinated minority, researchers would need a far more complex research design than any yet attempted. We would have to place a sample of black infant twins for adoption, one from each pair into a white household and the other into a black household. Then we would do the same for a sample of white twins, half in white households and half in black households. Then, to control for the possible social rejection of transracial fostering, we would have to change the color of the white twins to black and the color of the black twins to white. Needless to say, this research is not likely to be funded in the foreseeable future.

One classic study by psychologists Sandra Scarr and Richard Weinberg (1976) did compare the IQ scores of black children who had been adopted by affluent white foster parents with the test scores of white children who had been adopted and brought up by the same foster parents as the black children. In these affluent families, both black and white, adopted children at age seven scored higher than the general population. This can be taken as evidence that children in advantaged households have a head start over children in disadvantaged households. Furthermore, the IQs of these seven year olds were statistically the same for blacks and whites. When their IQs were tested ten years later, however, the black children's scores had regressed to the average black American score (i.e., fifteen points below the whites)

Clearly, the conditions of this study fall far short of controlling for black and white social experiences. The black children had already been handicapped before adoption by having been raised in inferior orphanages. They also had lived in orphanages for a longer period than the white children before being adopted. As they reached adolescence, the advantages they enjoyed by being brought up in protective and affluent white households gradually were outweighed by the increasing discrimination and racism they encountered outside of the home (Weinberg et al. 1992).

Other studies show that raciological explanations of low IQ scores represent a case of blaming the victim. Greg Duncan (et al. 1993) matched low-birth-weight black and white children who had experienced persistent poverty from birth to five years of age and found that both groups had IQs that were nine points lower than children who had low birth weights but no experience of persistent poverty. Their conclusion was that poverty had more influence on the IQs of these children than family structure or the educational level of the mother.

The Flynn Effect

Meanwhile, a startling new discovery called the Flynn effect has come along to challenge the basic premise that IQ scores measure a hereditary trait that is fixed and unchanging for a person's lifetime and that cannot be substantially modified by the learning environment. While studying intelligence testing in the U.S. military, psychologist James R. Flynn noticed that recruits who were average in comparison with their contemporaries were above average when compared with previous generations of recruits. The scores of different generations of recruits who took exactly the same tests have increased by about three points per decade. Twenty other countries for which data were available showed the same improvement. If IQ tests actually measure general intelligence, one would have to conclude that children being born today are 25 percent smarter than their grandparents (Horgan 1995; Neisser 1998). In any event, the Flynn effect occurs much too rapidly to be explained by genetic processes which would require many generations for their spread.

The causes of the Flynn effect are not well understood. It seems likely that the social environment created by postindustrial (I prefer the term "hyperindustrial") modes of communication and production has improved the overall quality of the social and economic environment for learning in technologically advanced fields. Students are better prepared to take tests of all sorts by being exposed to tests and test-like conditions at an early age.

While both blacks and whites experience the Flynn effect, they improved their scores at the same rate, resulting in the continuation of the fifteen-point difference. But the gap need not be permanent. Flynn suggests that if blacks in 1995 had the same score as whites had in 1945, it is likely that the average black environment of 1995 was equivalent in quality to the average white environment of 1945.

IQ STUDIES AND POLITICS

The idea that intelligence tests measure a heritable entity called G (for general intelligence) whose distribution varies across race and sex independently of sociocultural and other environmental conditioning has proven to be irresistible. In the 1970s and 1980s, IQ hereditarians and raciologists such as Arthur Jensen, Richard Herrnstein, Hans Eysenck, Audrey Shuey, and William Shockley, to mention only a few, played an important role in the formation of the white backlash to civil rights. An entire 123-page article by Jensen, *How Much Can We Boost IQ and Scholastic Achievement* (1969), was read into the *Congressional Record* and discussed by Richard Nixon's Cabinet (Lieberman and Kirk 1997:35).

The political significance of Jensenism was quite clear: compensatory education and affirmative action were useless because most of the economic and social gap between whites and blacks is caused by unalterable hereditary differences in intelligence. Psychologists dominated the ensuing debates, while anthropologists seemed conspicuous by their absence. During this period—the 1970s through the 1980s—many anthropologists, as we have seen, no doubt disengaged themselves because they believed that races did not exist except in an emic sense, and therefore were not worthy of serious discussion.

Jensen's ideas, slightly modified, enjoyed a new peak of popular and scientific approval. They were linked to the resurgence of the century-old attempt to apply Darwinian principles to the explanation of sociocultural evolution and to the election in 1994 of the most conservative Congress in more than sixty years.

Chapter 8

Neo-Darwinism

NEO-DARWINISM AND CULTURAL SELECTION

I should make it clear at the outset that the biologizing characteristic of neo-Darwinians does not necessarily involve raciological assumptions or theories. Nor are neo-Darwinists necessarily committed to the use of IQ tests as an explanatory principle. They nonetheless are responsible for one of the most vigorous and formidable challenges to the Boasian separation of culture from natural selection.

Neo-Darwinism comes in several different flavors. Its formative impulse dates to the 1970s and 1980s, with the work of E. O. Wilson. Wilson and his followers promoted a form of hereditarian discourse known as sociobiology, which emphasizes universal, genetically controlled cultural tendencies arising from human nature. Other early figures, such as biologist Richard Alexander and anthropologists Christine Hawkes, Bruce Smith, and Eric Winterhalder, have sought to separate their work from sociobiological inquiries about human nature, emphasizing instead the explanation of variations in human behavior resulting from evolutionary change using models derived from evolutionary ecology. Much of Wilson's original formulations have fallen into disuse within neo-Darwinian circles, and several alternative definitions and research directions are under discussion. As a sign of current trends, the *Journal of Ethology and Sociobiology* has had its name changed to *Evolution and Human Behavior*. An influential volume edited by Smith and Winterhalder (1992) bears the title *Evolutionary Ecology and Human Behavior*, carefully avoiding any mention of sociobiology. Meanwhile, a closely related field calling itself "evolutionary psychology" has been featured in *Time* magazine (Wright 1995) and in *Skeptic Magazine* (4(1):42ff). Writing in *Scientific American*, John Horgan (1995:174–81) notes "the astonishing ambition of the new social Darwinists." He reports that at the 1996 meetings of the Human Behavior and Evolution Society, there "was much gleeful bashing of those deluded souls who think culture—whatever that is—determines human behavior. . . . When anthropologist Lee Cronk derides cultural determinism [as opposed to biological determinism] as a religion rather than a rational stance, his audience roared with laughter."

The post-Wilsonian neo-Darwinians seek to explain variations in human behavior by studying the contribution that particular behaviors make to the propagation of an individual's genes across the generations. Variations that confer relatively greater fitness (i.e., reproductive success)—inclusive of the reproductive rates of near relatives—get selected for; those with relatively less fitness get selected against. For example, a neo-Darwinian explanation for laws that favor a sovereign's ability to become rich and powerful is that being rich and powerful leads to more opportunities for sexual intercourse and hence to greater reproductive success.

I have three main objections to popular current forms of neo-Darwinian theories of culture. The first is that cultural selection often does not favor behavioral and ideational innovations that increase reproductive success. The second is that reproductive success (even if it could be shown theoretically to control cultural selection) is almost impossible to measure in human populations. And the third is that, for every neo-Darwinist explanation, there is a cultural-materialist explanation that is more parsimonious and that does not require data on reproductive success.

Cultural Selection Does Not Always Favor Reproductive Success

Demographic phenomena are a source of refractory problems surrounding reproductive success. Neo-Darwinist theory predicts that the higher the income and the greater the disposable wealth, the greater the number of children per family. But it is generally accepted, contra the neo-Darwinists, that in the short run at least, poor couples have on the average more children than wealthy ones (Vining 1985). Remember that this fact—"inferiors" outbreeding "superiors"—was what motivated an earlier generation of hereditarians to start the eugenics movement. The neo-Darwinists have tried to deal with the same conundrum by proposing that eventually, in the long run, wealthy couples will outbreed poorer couples. This effect will take place because the descendants of the poorer couples will not be able to obtain sufficient resources to sustain their high rate of reproduction, whereas the wealthy couples will continue to support all their descendants. Since we are not told how long one must wait for the rate of reproduction of the wealthy to overtake that of the poor, we are left at best with an untestable hypothesis.

The case for long-run reproductive advantages of wealthy people has been studied by neo-Darwinist and anthropologist Alan Rogers (1992:399), using a mathematical model. Reversing an earlier study, Rogers states that, if the available data are correct, "The poor have greater reproductive success even in the long run." Bereft of a plausible explanation for this phenomenon, Rogers in effect concedes that the reproductive success model is not applicable to modern conditions:

> Perhaps we behave in ways that increased the reproductive
> success of our ancestors, but no longer do so today. If so,
> evolutionary theory will still be useful in discovering why
> the human mind has evolved into its present form, but we
> should not expect humans to maximize reproductive
> success in modern environments. (1992:400)

But it is not merely in modern environments that the principle of maximizing reproductive success does not apply. In many parts of Eurasia, elite classes and castes practice female infanticide, thereby reducing rather than increasing reproductive success, even though they possess the resources needed for rearing additional daughters. This practice is a culturally selected stratagem for conserving a family's wealth and power. Polyandry (marriage of one woman to several men, usually brothers) achieves a similar result; it limits the number of reproductive women and prevents the breakup of a wealthy family's farmlands (Levine 1988).

Male primogeniture, formerly common in Europe, is yet another stratagem that conserves the concentration of wealth and power and that is readily explicable in terms of limiting, rather than maximizing, reproductive success. Primogeniture, which gave control of the family estate to the firstborn son, was closely linked to the development of monasteries and seminaries, to which the junior members of the family could retreat to live nonreproductive lives.

Finally, there is the widespread practice, in industrial societies, of adoption, in which the adopting individuals have no kinship with the infants and children being adopted. Orphaned Russian children adopted by childless American couples can scarcely be said to be contributing to the enhancement of their foster parents' reproductive success. Rather, it is to the reproductive success of the completely unrelated biological father and mother to which the foster parents contribute. Some neo-Darwinists try to wriggle out of this conundrum by postulating an instinct for parenting that is supposedly part of human nature: the desire to raise children "is likely to be the product of evolved psychological predispositions that motivate us to cherish and protect children" (Boyd and Silk 1997:662). It would be nice if this theory were true, but the widespread practice of child abuse in contemporary industrial societies does not support it.

Given the fact that there are about four billion people living under "modern" or modernizing conditions, it seems to me that anthropologists ought not to rely on a research strategy whose central principle cannot be applied to the majority of people who have ever lived.

MEASURING REPRODUCTIVE SUCCESS

The second objection that I have to neo-Darwinian theories is that reproductive success is seldom directly measurable. Its putative effects are seen only through "proxies." In the words of anthropologist Raymond Hames (1992:204),

> Since fitness payoffs for alternative behaviors are practically
> impossible to measure, quantifiable measures . . . that
> correlate with fitness have been chosen.

The reason why fitness is impractical is spelled out by Eric Smith and
Bruce Winterhalder:

> Fitness offers the strongest deductive basis for ranking
> different outcomes in terms of selective value. But because
> it is a lifetime measure summing the effect of many
> different phenotypic characters, it is generally impractical
> as an empirical currency. (1992:55)

Similar observations have made their way into neo-Darwinist archaeology. Noting that it is "not possible to actually observe reproductive success in many real world situations," C. M. Barton and G. A. Clark opt for
a curious alternative definition of fitness:

> Fitness should be defined and measured in terms of
> successful information transmission—both potential and
> realized—rather than reproduction. (1997:12-3)

If a conundrum already exists in measuring reproductive success, it
boggles the mind to contemplate the dimensions of the conundrum involved in measuring "potential" information bearing on the transmission
of cultural innovations.

The proxies for measuring fitness payoffs most commonly employed
by ecological evolutionists are time, energy, and access to resources. The
unintended consequence of using these measures is that they suffice to
explain the behavior in question without invoking hypothetical reproductive advantages, but more about alternative explanations in a moment.

Evolutionary ecologists have put forward as their major achievement a series of studies that focus on time and energy expended in the

procurement of food among foragers (hunters and gatherers). In conformity with optimal foraging theory, as proposed by ecologists for nonhuman species, these studies reveal that, for the most part, foragers tend to
select those plant and animal species that yield, after encountering them,
the highest net energy return for the time spent in pursuing, preparing,
and processing them. Items that lower the average net energy return will
not be pursued regardless of their relative abundance in the habitat (Kaplan
and Hill 1992).

Evolutionary ecologists deserve to be roundly congratulated on the
numerous quantitative studies they have carried out to test and refine optimal foraging models among foraging cultures such as the Hadza of Tan-
zania, the Aché of Paraguay, and the San of Botswana. Their data on energy
costs and benefits are of enduring value. This achievement is marred, however, by the treatment of net energy costs and benefits as proxies for reproductive success, both in the absence of data on reproductive success and
despite the sufficient "costing" that energy budgets offer on their own.
The fact is that we do not know whether optimal foraging increases, de-
creases, or has no definite effect on reproductive success. What we do know
is that foragers (and probably humans in general) tend to economize; that
is, they will expend as little effort as possible to obtain as much of a desir-
able entity as possible. And this brings me to my third objection.

ALTERNATIVE THEORIES

Smith and Winterhalder (1992:xiii) describe what they are doing as "un-
leashing the power of Darwinism," but more parsimonious explanations
that do not involve an appeal to reproductive success are available in other
paradigms, especially in cultural materialism. For instance, consider the
explanation offered by anthropologist Mildred Dickeman (1979) for the
occurrence of female infanticide among elite classes and castes in late-
medieval Europe, India, and China. Dickeman relies on the model developed by Richard Alexander (1974), which predicts that female infanticide
is more likely in societies where women marry high-ranking men and less

likely in societies where women marry low-ranking men. The logic is this: when men can be confident that male infants will survive to adulthood, their fitness will tend to exceed that of females, since men can have many more reproductive episodes than women can have. Hence, where males have a good chance of surviving because their living conditions are excellent (when they are rich and powerful), the maximization of reproductive success of both male and female parents will be achieved by investing in sons rather than daughters. On the other hand, in low-ranking classes and castes, where male survival is very risky, reproductive success will be maximized by investing in daughters who are likely to have at least some reproductive episodes, rather than none at all.

A cultural materialist explanation for these phenomena begins with the observation that daughters were less valuable than sons among Eurasian elites because men dominated the political, military, commercial, and agricultural sources of wealth and power (for reasons that also can be best understood as cultural rather than biological selection). Sons, therefore, have the potential for protecting and enhancing an elite family's political-economic status. But daughters, who have access to wealth and power only through men (fathers, brothers, sons), are a burden; they subtract from, rather than add to, the wealth and power of their family. It is symptomatic of female status in many parts of Eurasia that families must provide their daughters with substantial dowries, usually moveable property, in order to marry them off as quickly as possible (hence, child brides in India and elsewhere in Eurasia). Under these circumstances, elite families will tend to practice female infanticide to avoid the expense of the dowry and to prevent the erosion of their wealth and power. The situation is quite different in the lower classes and castes. Female infanticide is not practiced as frequently as among the elites because women are not burdensome and contribute to their family income by working as farmers and cottage industry artisans.

The genesis of this system lies in the struggle to maintain and enhance differential politico-economic power and wealth, not in the struggle to achieve reproductive success. The proof of this lies in the very fact that female infanticide is practiced by groups that can well-afford to rear many more children than they actually raise. Like adoption, the practice of elite female infanticide defies explanation as a means of maximizing current inclusive fitness. I would argue that the entire system represents one of many cultural stratagems aimed at preventing too much reproductive success from eroding the privileged position of a small number of wealthy and powerful families at the top of the social pyramid.

Monique Borgerhoff Mulder (1992:356–7) provides a more bizarre example of a fixation on reproductive success to the exclusion of more parsimonious alternatives. She shows that women among the Kipsigis of East Africa prefer to marry men who have ample land to give them. The reason for this preference seems quite straightforward by the logic of cultural materialism. Land ownership is the key to Kipsigi prosperity, health, and many other kinds of benefits; thus the more land the better for the satisfaction of basic human needs and drives. But Mulder's explanation is that the preference for land ownership has been selected for because it provides more "breeding opportunities," and this in turn leads to reproductive success.

So ritualized is the appeal to reproductive success among evolutionary ecologists that, in a table showing the distribution of land among Kipsigi wives, Mulder includes a column entitled "Breeding Opportunity in Acres" (1992:357), as if the only significant advantage in controlling access to land is the opportunity it provides to have children.

A MISLEADING ANALOGY

The grand achievement of Boas and his followers was their rejection of Darwinian-Spencerian principles as a means of explaining the evolution of sociocultural differences and similarities. They were not opposed to the Darwinian understanding of descent with modification, natural selection, and the origin of species (a charge leveled against them by Boas's academic nemesis, Leslie White). Rather, they were simply opposed to the application of these bioevolutionary principles to culture. While the Boasians accomplished little by way of their own explanatory theories of culture, they nonetheless made their mark forever in establishing the ontological nature of human cultures as a quantitatively and qualitatively novel emergent feature of human social life. They saw more clearly than any before them that the separation of social learning from close genetic control constituted an event that was as momentous as the appearance of life out of matter. Thenceforth and to this day, every attempt to construe cultural selection as a form of natural selection is a step backwards. All attempts to use differential reproductive success—that is, Darwinian fitness—as the central explanatory feature of cultural anthropology are doomed to failure.

This is not to say that differential reproductive success has played no role in shaping cultural traditions. Instances such as the interplay between milk tolerance and dairying (Harris 1989), or between sickle-cell anemia and the anthropogenic expansion of habitats congenial to the anopheles mosquito, readily come to mind. The overwhelming majority of cultural innovations, however, do not get selected for or against as a result of their contribution to the reproductive success of the individuals who adopt the innovation. Edison's electric light bulbs did not spread around the world in twenty years because Edison or his relatives were reproductively more successful than people who used gaslight or kerosene lanterns. Indeed, electric lights spread laterally within a single generation among childless couples as rapidly as among couples who had children by the dozen.

This capacity for the lateral transmission of socially learned behaviors and thoughts is a distinctive attribute of cultural phenomena not found among nonhuman species, except in the most rudimentary form. True, sexually reproducing organisms exchange genes, but not genes for thoughts and behaviors acquired socially during an individual's lifetime. Many generations are required for genetically controlled innovative behaviors and thoughts to spread throughout a population and become part of the genome. New species (even under punctuated equilibrium scenarios) take on the order of hundreds of thousands or more years to evolve, whereas new societies and cultures appear and disappear on the order of, at most, a few thousand years.

The reason for the relatively slow tempo of biological evolution is that behavioral and ideational innovations must be encoded in the genes if they are to be preserved and propagated, and many reproductive episodes are required for this encoding to take place. Cultural evolution is not subject to any such restriction; cultural innovations are encoded not in the genes but in the brains and other neurosensory organs. This makes it possible for useful variations acquired during an individual's lifetime to be integrated directly into a population's behavioral repertory. But in biological evolution, there is no inheritance of acquired characteristics (although Darwin, along with Lamarck, thought otherwise).

The specific features of biological reproduction—the mechanics of meiosis, fertilization, and gestation—impose additional restrictions on biological evolution not encountered in the cultural realm. When organisms undergo bioevolutionary change, a point is reached beyond which they can no longer exchange genes. By contrast, no matter how culturally divergent any two human societies may become, they can always exchange cultural features (or the information necessary to construct such features). Alfred Kroeber (the most theoretically-minded of Boas's students) recognized the momentous significance of this difference in his depiction of what he called "the tree of life" and "the tree of culture"—one with the familiar trunk, branches, and twigs diverging in all directions; the other with branches and twigs growing back into each other (Kroeber 1948:200). A more appropriate depiction perhaps is that of a braided stream, in which the various currents diverge and merge to form a reticulate pattern (Moore 1994). As we shall see in a moment, the use of the tree-of-life model rather than the tree-of-culture model is a source of contention in the attempt to trace the origins of human ethnic groups.

≈

This categorical difference leads to certain expectations concerning the higher-order processes that govern the biological and cultural realms, respectively. Because of its tree-of-life pattern, we should, for example expect far more diversity in biological taxa than in sociocultural taxa. Indeed, there are about five thousand distinct cultures as compared with 1.75 million described biological species (many more remain to be described). In the construction of theoretical models, anthropologists can anticipate a far greater degree of convergence and parallelism in sociocultural evolution than in biological evolution.

To sum up, only by the wildest of imaginings can one draw a close analogy between biological and cultural evolution. True, both refer to continuity with change, the change of one form into another; but so does the evolution of stars into black holes, or tectonic plates into mountains. There is as little justification for applying Darwinian reproductive success to stellar or geological evolution as there is for applying it to cultural evolution.

Chapter 9

Confronting Ethnomania

America is awash with the imagery of bloodlines, ancestry, and roots. Everywhere there is talk of racial and ethnic identity, and of racial and ethnic pride, as the keys to personhood, mental maturity, healthy self-esteem, and social justice.

ETHNOMANIA

In the course of racial and ethnic politics, each group tends to pay far more attention to its own origins, history, heroism, suffering, and achievements than to those of other racial and ethnic groups. As a consequence, racist and ethnocentric fictions masquerade as educational reforms, such as when it is asserted that Egyptians are blacks or that the Greeks "stole" western culture from the Egyptians. The constructions of racial and ethnic ancestry employed by both dominant and dominated racial and ethnic groups seemingly deny that Gregor Mendel ever existed. Individuals, for example, who seek to identify themselves as "mixed" or "none of the above" or who try to "pass" are subject to vilification.

Blood is still widely regarded as the hereditary substance that defines ancestry (as opposed to DNA); the "one drop of blood" rule, as we have seen, still befuddles otherwise well-educated people. While some ethnic and racial leaders prattle on about preserving cultures that never existed, others offer theories that blame colonialism on the icy hearts of white men and that explain Negro jazz as the result of high levels of melanin.

Meanwhile, on most of the nation's campuses, segregation has become a matter of ethnic and racial groups keeping all others away, as much as one of all others keeping members of ethnic and racial groups away. In this context, ethnicity turns out to mean an especially aggressive and virulent form of ethnocentrism for which the term *ethnomania* seems appropriate.

Origins of Ethnomania

Ethnic identity is closely entwined with prehistoric fictions that were invented to hold human social groups together. At some point in the evolution of *Homo sapiens*, between 200,000 and 100,000 years ago, our ancestors reached a level of linguistic competence that enabled them to theorize about the world and to explain it to each other. One of the earliest kinds of stories that people told must have involved explanations of the social order in which they found themselves living. On the basis of chimpanzee and other primate models, we can be quite certain that social order came first and the explanations later, for these cousin-species have a complex and coherent social life without benefit of developed languages.

Our early ancestors had no need for explanations. It is only with the gift of language that one becomes interested in the question of who we are and why we are living together. Of course, no one knows precisely what the content of these first glimmerings of questions and answers were like, but there can be little doubt that they soon led to one of the most powerful and treacherous intellectual constructions of all time. I refer to the invention of the concept of descent, the principle whereby individuals and groups establish their identities or relatedness. Although theories of descent vary from culture to culture, the basic idea occurs universally; namely that individuals must acknowledge a special relatedness to parents and to children that endures after death. Descent implies the preservation of some aspect of the substance or spirit of people in past and future generations and thus is a symbolic form of immortality. Descent lies at the heart of the problem both of identity and of the formation of ethnic and racial groups, as well as of all that connects or ties relatives (kin) together.

DESCENT AND SOCIAL RACES

Social races are emic groups whose members believe themselves or others to be physically and psychologically alike as a consequence of common descent. Various systems for identifying social races are in use throughout the world today. In the United States, African Americans (blacks) identify themselves and are identified by others as a distinct social race primarily on the basis of their skin color. Reliance on this principle alone, however, would leave the identity of millions of people in doubt because skin color (and other "African" and "Caucasian" traits) varies across a broad spectrum of nuanced differences, from very dark to brown to very light, as a result of recent interracial matings and marriages.

In the context of slavery and its aftermath, when it was official policy to discriminate against blacks, some rule or principle was needed to categorize people as either black or white so that the discriminatory measures would be applied to blacks who looked like whites but not to whites who looked like blacks. To solve this quandary, the "one drop" rule was constructed: blacks are anyone who has the slightest amount of black "blood," as attested to by their having even one ancestor who is known to have been identified as black (whether or not this ancestor himself or herself was also a child of a mixed marriage or mating). By the "one drop" rule, which is still in force today, children of a mixed marriage between one biologically white and one biologically black parent are socially black; but as previously indicated, the etic reality is that all of us inherit half of our nuclear genes from mother and half from father.

A very different construction of social race prevails in Latin America and the Caribbean Islands. In Brazil, for example, racial categorizations depend mainly on the perceptions that people have of each other's appearance, with equal emphasis on skin color and hair form. A person's "racial" identity may also be influenced by his or her wealth and profession. A surprising number of different terms are available for identifying any individual's particular combination of traits (in one study, 492 different terms were encountered). The "one drop" rule doesn't exist in Brazil; ancestry or descent is not important for racial identity. This means that children can have a racial identity that is different from that of their parents and further that one child can be identified as "white," while his or her full brother or sister can be identified as "black."

ETHNICITY

Ethnic groups define themselves (or are defined by others) in a manner that closely resembles the way social races are defined. In fact, it may be difficult to decide whether a particular population is a social race or an ethnic group. Members of ethnic groups often believe that they have a distinctive appearance, that they are descended from common ancestors, and that they share distinctive traditions and customs. Some ethnic groups, like the "white ethnics" (Irish Americans, Italian Americans, Polish Americans, Jewish Americans, Greek Americans, etc.) in the United States, see themselves as divisions or branches of a single social race. But other ethnic groups (e.g., Cubans in Miami; Haitians in New York) may themselves recognize that they are not racially homogeneous.

The difference between social race and ethnicity comes down to the relative weight given to cultural commonalities as opposed to common descent or physical appearance. Ethnicity is believed to be associated with distinctive cuisines, holidays, religious beliefs, dances, folklore, dress, and other traditions, but the single most powerful cultural source of ethnic identity is the possession of a common language or dialect. Use of a common language or dialect instills a sense of community that is powerful enough to override social race, differences of class, and the absence of any other kinds of cultural traditions.

The emergence of the ethnic category "Hispanic" in the United States illustrates this point. Hispanics include people who are recent immigrants from Spain, from the Spanish-speaking Caribbean islands, and from various parts of Mexico and Central and South America, plus descendents of the Spanish-speaking settlers in the West and Southwest. The cultures of Hispanic Americans, with the exception of their common language, differ at least as much as the cultures of Polish Americans and Italian Americans differ from each other.

THE STRUGGLE FOR ETHNIC AND RACIAL EMPOWERMENT

In a democracy, only those who speak up are heard; and friendly outsiders alone never provide a secure power base. Translated into the nitty-gritty of racial and ethnic politics, this means that for empowerment, each group needs both to learn to speak loudly in its own voice and to rely primarily on its own material and ideological resources. In the late 1960s, these principles made it easy for white liberals to step aside as various power movements—black, red, brown, and yellow—set about creating the world in their respective images.

Wars and migration have been the major sources of the ethnic and racial diversity we see around us. Captured and enslaved African peoples were transported against their will across the ocean, while Native Americans, defeated in their attempt to safeguard their homelands, were forced to migrate to distant reservations. Conquest also lies at the root of the Hispanic ethnic group in the Southwest and in California. Meanwhile, white ethnics, especially those from Ireland and from eastern and southern Europe migrated under various degrees of compulsion in search of relief from religious or political persecution, military impressment, economic insolvency, and the threat of outright starvation. While each ethnic group has its distinctive history, they all share many experiences and have evolved along similar lines in response to similar pressures. Most of them started out low in the social and economic hierarchy and have struggled to gain respect and to increase their access to local and national sources of wealth and power.

To be sure, some groups were better prepared by their own cultural traditions to cope with the challenges of their new conditions of life. Those with strong literate traditions were preadapted for competing in the rapidly changing world of an urban industrial society. Knowledge of English was usually indispensable for success in this effort, leading to the gradual disuse and abandonment of ethnic native languages by the majority of white ethnics. Other pressures have led white ethnics to abandon a large part of their native cuisine and many of their other distinctive cultural traditions. Does this mean that white ethnic groups are blending into a single white social race, as in the theory of the melting pot? Yes and no. The evidence is equivocal. There is an ongoing effort to promote ethnic pride and to revitalize old ethnic traditions, or to invent new ones.

But the lifestyles of white Americans have become so homogeneous that young people from different ethnic groups are finding it increasingly acceptable to marry each other. In the absence of a rigid rule of descent (like the "one drop" rule), the ethnic identity of children and grandchildren of ethnically mixed marriages tends to grow weaker and to become more a matter of choice than of ascription. To combat these trends, white ethnics are massaging their own racial and ethnic identities. In unprecedented numbers during the 1980s and 1990s, they have taken up the study of languages spoken by their grandparents, promoted public festivals and parades to celebrate their cultural traditions, established various single-group ethnic defense funds, and vigorously campaigned to block or reverse affirmative action policies designed to help nonwhites.

Although the sense of having a distinctive culture is important in order to mobilize resistance within disadvantaged social races and ethnic groups, a rigid linking of race or ethnic group to culture is a form of racism that runs counter to all that is known about the transmissibility of cultures across racial and ethnic boundaries. At birth, every healthy human infant, regardless of race or ethnicity, has the capacity to acquire the traditions, practices, values, and languages found in any of the world's five thousand or so different cultures.

AFROCENTRIC ETHNOMANIA

What began as an argument for equality has escalated into an argument for supremacy. Leaders of nonwhite power movements now urge their followers to think of themselves as *more* beautiful, intelligent, musical, athletic, generous, earth-caring, and human than people of European descent. These African American leaders warn that whites are full of psychological hang-ups that blacks do not have: Blacks should come to their senses and stop envying whites and seeking their company. They should stop trying to "act white" (which, sadly enough, often means not striving to get good grades), and they should avoid sex and marriage with white partners.

African Americans have been confronted with some of the same pressures and alternatives as white ethnics, having lost most of their African cultural heritages as well as their knowledge of ancestral languages. Like white ethnics, they have sought to increase their sense of unity and identity by revitalizing old and inventing new cultural traditions. Unlike white ethnics, however, they have never had the option of blending in with the rest of the population. Because of the "one drop" rule, intermarriage does not lead to any modification in allowable identities. In any event, black/white intermarriage is rare and subject to criticism from both whites and blacks. Under these circumstances, it is understandable why African Americans have turned their attention away from assimilation and redoubled their efforts to instill pride in being black, emphasizing real or imagined cultural achievements.

Black American scholars, authors and radio talk-show hosts urge people of African descent to see the world through African American eyes. They must learn to be Afrocentric, which means they must stop believing history as recounted by white historians and believe history only as recounted by black Afrocentric historians.

INVENTING AFRICAN HISTORY

One of the principal objectives of Afrocentrism is the inculcation of respect for black Africa's history. White scholars allegedly have conspired to make it seem as if black Africans have never made any significant contribution to civilization. White scholars allegedly lie when they attribute the foundations of European science, philosophy, and art to the ancient Greeks.

On the contrary, argue the Afrocentrists, the Greeks "stole" civilization from the Egyptians. And the Egyptians, including the pharaohs and even Cleopatra, were not whites, as white historians would have everyone believe, but black. Black intelligence must therefore be credited with most of the foundational achievements that white historians generally attribute to Greeks and other Europeans.

Not only did black Egyptians invent writing, astronomy, mathematics, and philosophy, but their genius was so advanced they were able to make the first electrochemical storage batteries, plus the first airplanes to be used for "travel, expeditions, and recreation" (Adams 1990:S-53).

Dubious claims about Egyptian "firsts" are scarcely needed to establish the advanced nature of ancient Egypt's arts, crafts, and technology. The Afrocentrist point, however, is not simply that the Egyptians were as inventive and intelligent as Europeans. Rather the point is that they were *more* inventive and intelligent than Europeans and that Europe owes its own belated advances toward civilization to black Africans.

Much can be said in favor of the Afrocentrist attempt to draw attention to non-Hellenic influences on the development of European cultures. Many old-style classicists did tend to disregard the 2,500 years during which Egypt had flourished as a huge imperial state while the Greeks remained a collection of petty chiefdoms. But the notion that the Greeks "stole" substantial parts of their culture from the Egyptians or anyone else is ethnomaniacal theater.

THE STOLEN-CULTURE MYTH

There are two fundamental processes that participate in shaping cultural differences and similarities. One is independent invention; the other is diffusion. The Native American domestication of plants and animals using wild species that occur only in the Americas is a case of independent invention. So, too, is the political system known as chiefdoms that recurrently evolved in different parts of the world among societies that were isolated from each other. An example of the other process—diffusion—is the spread of New World crops such as potatoes, tomatoes, and maize from their cultures of origin to other cultures, near and far. So, too, is the spread of religions like Christianity and Islam from their original homelands.

It is diffusion from Egypt to Greece that accounts for most of the similarities in Greek and Egyptian cultures. In the majority of instances, especially in preindustrial and precapitalist times, diffusion has nothing to do with stealthy expropriation, as implied in the concept of culture being stolen. (Migration, conquest, trade, and intermarriage are some of the more common modes of diffusion.) Moreover, Egypt was not the only source of the complex urban and imperial cultural achievements that influenced the Greeks. Many archaeologists consider the civilizations of Mesopotamia to be at least as important as that of Egypt in influencing the subsequent development of Greece and Europe. (The Babylonians, for example, produced the first written code of laws.)

Ignoring the influence of Mesopotamia, and labeling diffusion from Egypt to Greece "theft," undermines our ability to understand history and cultural evolution. All cultures consist of a melange of elements derived from other cultures as a result of direct or indirect contact and diffusion, and this holds as much for Egyptian as for Greek culture. Indeed the more developed and complex a society is, the more its culture (and subcultures) will reflect the influence of near and distant diffusionary contacts and the greater in turn will be that society's cultural influence. That is the lesson that needs to be taught in the name of multiculturalism, not the ethnomaniacal idea that Greeks stole philosophy and mathematics from black Africans.

EGYPTIAN COLORS

Afrocentric fanfares for Egypt serve the Afrocentric cause only if the ancient Egyptians were black. Were they? (Curiously, it sometimes seems as if Afrocentrists argue that since Egypt is in Africa, its inhabitants must be Africans.)

Evidence from mummies, paintings, sculpture, and inscriptions supports the conclusion that the ancient distribution of racial types in Egypt was similar to what can be seen in Egypt today. Northern Egyptians are predominantly light-skinned and have straight to wavy hair. As one proceeds up the Nile, skin colors darken and there is a greater incidence of tightly curled hair, broad noses, and thick lips. Above Aswan, in the First Cataract region, black African individuals become common. The Egyptian people therefore cannot be said to be either white or black; they are a mixture of at least two major populations who were exchanging genes long before the first pyramids were built (Brace 1993).

Direct inspection of the royal mummies confirms the diversity of types in Dynastic times. Pharaoh Rameses II, who came from the extreme north, had fine wavy hair, a prominent hooked nose, and moderately thin lips (Yurco 1989:25). But the mummy of Seyenen-Re Tao, who was from Thebes, further south, had tightly curled hair and Nubian facial features. As for Cleopatra, it is extremely unlikely that she looked like a black African. Her family, the Ptolemies, who conquered Egypt in the early fourth century B.C., was Macedonian Greek and was known for its intense devotion to Greek culture. Like a number of other extremely powerful dynastic families around the world, the Ptolemies practiced a form of brother-sister marriage; they had been doing this for eleven generations before the birth of Cleopatra. While it is true that Cleopatra's grandmother was a royal concubine, the Ptolemies favored mistresses who had Greek ancestors (Yurco 1989).

WHY AFRICA LAGS

Whether or not the ancient Egyptians were black, we are left with the problem of why other regions of Africa present much less precocious histories. The deficits are well-marked in the lands south of the Sahara where the highest concentrations of people with very dark, negroid features occur. Throughout this region, the development of complex states, writing, mathematics, astronomy, and monumental architecture lagged far behind the pace of developments in Egypt, Mesopotamia, the Indus Valley, and China, which were the earliest centers of state formation in the Old World. And this region was also the homeland of most of the slaves who were brought to the Americas.

If black Africa did, in fact, lag behind the earliest centers of imperial development, is that a reason to conclude that black Africans were or are genetically inferior? It seems far more important to understand why no such conclusion can be reached than it is to deny that the question needs an answer by including Egypt in black Africa. (That gambit resembles the proposal to combat racism by denying that races exist.) White Europe, in the north and west, was also a laggard, as attested to by the Roman belief that the inhabitants of the British Isles, whom they had conquered, were so little civilized that they excelled only at being slaves.

Different rates and directions of cultural change found in different times and places result in laggards becoming leaders and leaders becoming laggards (or conquerors being conquered and vice versa). There is no way to accommodate the ups and downs of history in racist theories without turning genes on and off in defiance of the laws of heredity. In contrast, cultural adaptations readily account for historical ups and downs. Geography and ecology, not race, explain why when Stonehenge, the largest megalithic construction in Great Britain, was completed at about 1100 B.C., the Great Pyramid of Cheops already had been standing for 1700 years. The precocious developments in Egypt, Mesopotamia, India, and China owe much to their location in great fertile river valleys surrounded by arid lands unsuited for agriculture and to their populations' dependence upon government-controlled massive irrigation works. States that developed outside of these centers were limited not by racial endowments, but by radically different forms of cultural-ecological adaptations involving decentralized forms of rainfall agriculture. Later, it was precisely the smaller, decentralized states that gave rise to capitalism and the industrial revolution—more about this in chapter 13.

The Development of Underdevelopment

Between A.D. 500 and 1200, feudal kingdoms flourished in both West Africa and Western Europe, roughly at similar levels of complexity. No amount of Afrocentric hyperbole can erase the fact that Western Europe thereafter developed more rapidly from the point of view of technology, military power, and scientific knowledge. Again, geography and ecology readily account for the different rates of development. The presence of the tsetse fly throughout the forested regions of Africa south of the Sahara meant that cattle and other domesticated animals could not be used as a source of traction power and dairying. Without traction animals, hoes rather than plows remained the chief agricultural implements. Horses, which became the chief engines of warfare in medieval Europe, were scarce or absent in tropical Africa.

While the people who lived in the Mediterranean basin carried out their trade and warfare on ships and became maritime powers, their black counterparts south of the Sahara were mainly concerned with crossing the desert and lacked any motivation for maritime adventures. The first Portuguese ships arrived off the Guinea coast in the fifteenth century and quickly seized control of the natural harbors, sealing the fate of Africa for the next five hundred years. Gold was the first export, but when the mines ran out the slave trade proved to be even more profitable. The Europeans depended on African slave hunters, paying them with firearms and cloth. Soon vast portions of the interior were turned into the breeding grounds of a human crop destined to be sent to the sugar, cotton, and tobacco plantations on the other side of the Atlantic.

Incidentally, Afrocentrists claim that Africans knew nothing of slavery until the Europeans arrived; but some form of slavery existed wherever chiefdoms or ancient states developed—which means on every continent except Australia. Neither the Arabs nor the Europeans were responsible for introducing slavery into Africa. What the Europeans did was to turn African slave-raiding into an industry unprecedented in its scope and ferocity. They could not have done this, however, without the help of African slavers who were driven by the same greedy demons that drove the whites.

With the end of the slave trade, the Europeans turned to new schemes for extracting wealth from Africa that did not require shipping the labor force across the ocean. Colonial labor laws drove Africans off the land and into low-wage migratory employment in mines and European-owned plantations. Meanwhile, the colonial authorities made every effort to keep Africa subservient and backward by encouraging ethnic wars, by limiting education to rudimentary schools, and above all by preventing colonies from developing an industrial infrastructure that might have made it possible to compete on the world market after they achieved political independence. Whether ancient Egypt was black or white, nothing can alter the fact that it was the Europeans, with their advanced military and maritime technologies, who achieved dominion over the Africans. Pointing to the triumphs of an ancient black Egypt, even if it existed, explains not a jot of what happened in Africa during the period of European colonialism and imperialism. All it does is lend credence to the all-too-widely held belief that race explains why most of the poorest and least-industrialized nations in the world are found in black Africa.

MELANIN THEORY

Afrocentric versions of the origins of civilization do not lack for ingenious explanations of how heredity produces its effects on history and culture. The burden of explaining the link between biology and culture falls on "melanin theory," according to which the pigment melanin not only controls skin color and protects against solar radiation, but bestows special powers that are proportionate to the density of an individual's melanin supply. This supply is allegedly present both in the melanocyte cells of the skin and muscles, and in the form of neuromelanin in the brain.

Melanin in the skin and muscles acts like a semiconductor. It traps free energy from the environment and thus accounts for the extra speed and agility of black athletes. Neuromelanin stimulates the immune system, expands memory and consciousness, and gives rise to higher forms of spirituality that we call "soul." Jazz and similar musical styles, and religious forms of expression involving "shouting" and "speaking in tongues," derive from neuromelanin-induced spirituality.

Neuromelanin can also pick up and decode cosmic rays and act as an infrared telescope. This accounts for the amazing knowledge that the people of the Dogon region of West Africa possessed concerning the existence of a companion star of Sirius that is invisible to the naked eye and that European astronomers found out about only after they had telescopes. It is no exaggeration to say that the development of all life was dependent on melanin and that possession of melanin defines the very essence of humanity: to be human is to be black.

Melanin, however, cannot be responsible for athletic prowess because it does not occur in muscle tissue (although it could conceivably have an effect on visual acuity). While melanin does occur in the human brain as neuromelanin, it forms as a byproduct in the biosynthesis of adrenaline and has no known function. In any event, according to Bernard Ortiz de Montellano (1993), there is absolutely no correlation between the amount of neuromelanin (which simply increases with age) and the amount of skin melanin (whose abundance is regulated by the enzyme tyrosinase). Therefore, all of the effects attributed to neuromelanin, such as musical ability and "soulful" spirituality, should be as common among whites as among blacks. As for the amazing discovery of the companion star of Sirius, restudies carried out by Walter van Beek (1991:148) cast much that had been written about Dogon religion and world view into doubt: "That Sirius is a double star is unknown [among the people of the region]; astronomy is of very little importance in [Dogon] religion." Finally, it is difficult to identify melanin as the primordial source of life. As Ortiz de Montellano (1993) notes, life began in the sea, the waters of which provided protection against solar radiation in the absence of melanin.

ALBINO THEORY

Other branches of melanin theory start from the proposition that the ancestors of whites were black Africans, and that, as a result of a mutation, certain individuals became albinos. Revolted by what they saw, blacks drove the white albino mutants from their African paradise. Ever since they became albino mutants, whites have been psychologically obsessed with their loss of melanin—witness their efforts to brown their skin even at the risk of getting cancer and the male whites' love of big black cigars. Even the white religion of Christianity is a reaction to mutant albinism. Christ was a poor black African who threatened to get out of control and "genetically annihilate" the white Romans. So they hung him on the cross, which the white male psyche had invented and which symbolically represented the black male's genitals.

> In other words, the white brain-computer that feared
> annihilation by the Black male genitals subconsciously
> invented an instrument or weapon of Black male
> destruction, exactly (in abstract form) analogous to the
> part of the Black male's anatomy that whites knew could
> destroy them. (Welsing 1991:74)

Then the mutant albino Christians tried to devise a ritual that would compensate for their race inferiority. Thus emerged the symbolic and ritualized acts of ingesting the body and blood (genes) of Jesus, the black African male in the rite of the Eucharist.

Despite their pariah status, the albino white mutants possess a burning desire to "survive as a global minority." Everything they think and do has the same bottom line: "genetic survival." Consciously or subconsciously, the albino mutants know that people who possess melanin have the biological capacity to outbreed and destroy them. Blacks will always be superior to the white albino mutants because the (hue)mans (sic) outnumber them and have something the whites can never get. It is the white's reproductive inadequacy and color deficiency that explains the racist themes of western civilization. The global patterns of racism are a survival necessity for the white collective:

> A compensatory attempt to prevent white genetic
> annihilation on a planet where the vast majority of peoples
> are genetically dominant to the melanin-deficient whites.

Or so opines African American psychiatrist Francis Welsing (1991:44).

Reality check: Albinism is a condition that occurs when both parents posses a single mutant gene that blocks the synthesis of melanin in the skin, hair, and iris. Normal skin color is controlled by an estimated four to six different genes; their joint action results in the complex patterns of intermediate shades and hues that characterize most large human populations. All normal whites possess as many melanocytes—melanin-producing cells—as blacks. What they have in lesser degree than blacks is tyrosinase, the enzyme that stimulates the melanocytes to synthesize melanin. Nonetheless, as Welsing observes, the majority of whites can produce enough melanin to get quite tan in the sun.

Welsing believes whites are possessed by a demonic urge to avoid becoming genetically extinct, and this leads to a struggle for survival that, we are told, the whites cannot win. Welsing has as little evidence for a collective racial consciousness and struggle for survival as did the Nazis, who postulated the same kind of consciousness for Aryans while carrying out a race war against Jews, Gypsies, and other "defective" types. The rebuttal of these postulated instinctual drives to preserve the race lies in evidence closer at hand, however. One need merely reflect on the predominance of brown skin color over very white or very black in the world today. If the races are involved in wars to preserve their identity, how can we account for the genetically mixed populations of India, Southeast Asia, the Caribbean, Mexico, and Brazil, not to mention Egypt and the United States?

ICEMAN THEORY

Albino mutation is not the only available explanation for the origin of the melanin-deficient, defective, pariah white race. Also popular among Afrocentrists is the iceman theory, first presented by Michael Bradley in a 1978 book entitled *The Iceman Inheritance: Prehistoric Sources of Western Man's Racism, Sexism and Aggression*. Although Bradley is white, his work has been endorsed by Afrocentric luminaries such as Leonard Jeffries, chair of the Black Studies Department at the City College of New York.

The iceman theory holds that the racial characteristics of whites are different from those of blacks because the ancestors of today's whites belonged to a separate branch of the human species: the Neandertals. These cold-adapted quasi-human creatures spent the ice age living amid glaciers in damp, sunless caves. To withstand the freezing temperatures, Neandertals had to retain a hairy coat, thicker for males than for females. Furthermore, Neandertal women were very plump to conserve heat. Because they looked so different, the sexes could not trust each other. Their alienation increased because the hairy coat diminished the tactile stimulation enjoyed by warm-climate humans. At the same time, "in the interests of cold-weather survival, Neandertals could not sport vulnerable extremities" (Bradley 1978:122). So their penises became smaller. Their sex lives were very frustrating, which made them more aggressive and cruel than the other races:

> a uniquely alienated creature, a figure uniquely conscious
> of physical differences among people . . . and distrustful of
> those differences. (124)

Because the ancestors of Europeans were brought up in caves, their descendants are cold, individualistic, materialistic, and aggressive individuals who have brought the world the three Ds: domination, destruction, and death. In contrast, Africans are warm, humanistic, and communitarian (Schlesinger 1992:67–8).

Why there should be a genetic link between skin color and psychological tendencies is difficult to imagine. Skin color is an adaptive trait related to the problem of balancing the positive and negative effects of solar radiation, which on the one hand can cause skin cancer and on the other can promote the synthesis of vitamin D. Cultural and natural selection favored white skin in northern habitats with weak solar radiation, where the danger humans confronted was not skin cancer from too little protective melanin, but rickets, hypocalcemia, and osteomalacia from too much protective melanin. No doubt cultural selection helped push the process along; as experience showed that light-colored individuals fared best in northern climes, they were given preferential treatment as babies and as mates. White became beautiful because white meant health and long life. Black was the color of death. In equatorial climes, it was dark skin that was equated with health and long life. Black was beautiful in babies and mates; and throughout West Africa, white was the color of the devil and death.

The iceman theory's postulated dehumanizing effects of a frigid homeland evoke memories of Nazi attempts to explain the origin of the Aryans. The Nazi's top racist ideologues, such as Alfred Rosenberg, concocted the story that the Aryan homeland had been the lost continent of Atlantis:

> A continent on which a creative race nurtured a great, far-
> reaching culture and sent its children out into the world as
> sea-voyagers. ([1930] 1970:38)

They then spread over Europe and North Africa, India and beyond:

> A blue-eyed, blond race which, in several massive waves,
> has determined the spiritual physiognomy of the world,
> while determining what aspects of it must perish.
> ([1930] 1970:38)

The Nazis praised the ice folk; the Afrocentrists condemn them. Otherwise, the Black and Aryan race myths share much in common. According to Rosenberg, the driving force of history was neither class struggle nor religion; it was rather "the conflict between blood and blood, race and race, people and people." Ranting about "race-soul," Rosenberg, who was hung as a war criminal, declared: "Soul means race viewed from within. And, vice versa, race is the externalization of soul." Substituting black soul for white soul does nothing to clarify these ethnomaniacal mystifications of the human condition.

∼

Martin Bernal, whose book *Black Athena* has been used by Afrocentrist extremists to bolster the claim that civilization began in black Africa, argues that racism directed against blacks is somehow worse than racism directed against whites.

> I hate racism of any kind, however I am infinitely less
> concerned by black racism than I am by white racism . . .
> (1991:xxii)

In view of the smoking ruins associated with race and ethnic confrontations from Los Angeles to Sarajevo, these sentiments seem deliberately provocative. If there is anything that the recent history of racial and ethnic conflict has to teach us, it is that ethnomania kills people, neighborhoods, communities, and whole societies.

Part III

Explanatory Principles

Chapter 10

Holism

It has long been an article of faith among anthropologists that our profession derives its claim to a distinctive space in academia because of its holistic approach. Robert Borofsky (1994:12–3), writes that the proposition "cultures need to be studied as wholes, not as fragmented pieces" forms part of the "shared traditions" that "hold cultural anthropology together." Who among us has not assured our introductory students that they have done the right thing in taking ANT 1001 because, unlike the heathen sociologists or historians, anthropologists possess the Holy Grail of holism? Unfortunately, as with so many precious gifts of the intellect, anthropologists do not agree on what holism is. There seem to be not one, but several different kinds of holistic approaches available to the social sciences. I can readily identify four of them: methodological holism, functionalist holism, laundry-list holism, and processual holism. I have already discussed the first of these in relation to methodological individualism and the existence of supraindividual sociocultural entities (chapter 3). The conclusion reached was that both individual entities and distinctively supraindividual entities have physical reality and thus a claim on our attention. I turn now to a discussion of the three remaining varieties of holism.

FUNCTIONALIST HOLISM

In the words of Webster's Third, holism is "the organic or functional relation between parts and wholes." If we change this slightly to read "between parts and parts, and parts and wholes," we get a definition of holism that has enjoyed considerable popularity among anthropologists for many years. Borofsky (1994:13) identifies this genre of holism as seeing cultural elements "as interrelated and interdependent." According to textbook authors Beals and Hoijer (1971:110), holism means that "the various aspects of culture are interrelated . . . they form systems whose parts or activities are directly or indirectly related to and affect one another." A similar definition of holism appears in William Haviland's (1993:13) introductory textbook:

> Only by discovering how all cultural institutions—social,
> political, economic, religious—relate to one another can
> the ethnographer begin to understand the cultural system.
> Anthropologists refer to this as the holistic perspective.

If we suppose that "relate to one another" includes "affect each other," then Haviland's definition of holism is very close to that of Beals and Hoijer. (There are additional ingredients in Haviland's and Beals and Hoijer's definitions that I will discuss in a moment.)

Functional holism does not require us to accept any of the dubious metaphysical propositions that characterize methodological holism. The whole is not greater than the sum of its parts; the whole does not determine the nature of its parts more than the nature of its parts determines the whole; and neither the parts nor the whole can be understood in isolation from each other. Best of all, one does not have to abandon the logical and empirical foundations of science in order to conduct research concerned with sociocultural phenomena. The problem with functional holism lies elsewhere. The organismic analogy on which it depends biases functional holism against evolutionary perspectives. It provides a kind of synchronic physiology of the social animal in which all the organs and cells work together harmoniously to maintain themselves without changing or evolving, but even small-scale band and village societies consist of parts—genders, families, age grades—whose conflicting interests are a source of dynamic tension that often leads to new social and cultural arrangements.

LAUNDRY-LIST HOLISM

This variety of holism refers to the breadth of topics (aspects, subjects) that anthropologists study. Logically, functional and laundry-list are not mutually exclusive; in fact, many anthropologists apparently see functional holism as the source of the uniquely wide breadth of holistic anthropology. As noted by Beals and Hoijer,

> In contrast to more specialized disciplines they [anthro-
> pologists] stress the study of the whole society. This
> position is possible because the various aspects of culture
> are interrelated.

Similarly, Haviland's functionalist definition quoted above refers to holism as a matter of paying attention to how "*all* cultural institutions . . . relate to each other" (emphasis added). In a sidebar definition, Haviland (1993:14) defines holistic perspective in laundry-list terms, but minus the reference to "all cultural institutions." Instead, he says holistic perspective is the "principle that things must be viewed in the broadest possible context."

Haviland is the author of a popular four-field text, so it is somewhat surprising that, in defining holism in terms of topical coverage, he omits any appeal to the archaeological, biological, and linguistic contexts that have traditionally added topical breadth to the teaching of anthropology. Perhaps the explanation for this omission lies in the conceptual priority bestowed on sociocultural systems by the social sciences. Functional analyses traditionally lie in the domains of institutions; the inertia of this position makes it difficult to reconcile functional holism with a topical holism in a manner that does justice to archaeological, linguistic, psychocultural, and biocultural studies.

A perusal of additional introductory texts suggests that laundry-list definitions of anthropological holism are gaining ground at the expense of definitions that focus on sociocultural integration. Nanda's (1991:5) "holistic approach" for example, includes the interaction of biology and culture, health and illness in the human body, speeches, and everyday conversation. For Howard and Dunaif-Hattis (1992:4), holism involves all aspects of the human condition, including a society's physical environment and its past as well as its present. Ember and Ember's (1990:3) holistic approach includes the physical characteristics of our prehistoric ancestors and the biological effects of the environment on a human population, while Kottak defines the thrust of anthropological holism as:

> anthropology's unique blend of biological, social, cultural, linguistic, historical and contemporary perspectives. . . . Holistic: Interested in the whole of the human condition: past, present, and future; biology, society, language, and culture. (1991:13;17)

Note that Kottak here comes close to defining anthropological holism as the famous "four field" approach. True, the word *archaeology* gets slighted, but one can easily interpret "historical" and the "past" as indicative of an archaeological component.

The troubling aspect of laundry-list definitions of holism is that they lack any internal or external logic suitable for explaining why one item is on the list and another is not. In the case of the four fields, for example, we know that we are dealing with a convention that reflects the outcome of various battles over academic turf at the beginning of the century, but the absence of psychology, ecology, and demography seems especially egregious in speaking of the "whole human condition." Furthermore, there is the question of the allocation of time and space to the various components. Haviland writes that we need to provide a broad view of culture "without emphasizing one of its parts to the detriment of another." But is this even theoretically possible, given the different professional experiences and paradigmatic commitments of authors and teachers? True, most popular textbooks cover a similar range of topics (allowing for the distinction between cultural and general versions), and they even display a considerable amount of similarity in emphasis. This similarity alone, however, is not a vindication of the laundry-list definition of holism; rather, it merely signifies that one of the first things that textbook publishers do is to make sure that all the topics that are prominent in the most popular texts are included in their own authors' works.

PROCESSUAL HOLISM

The escape from laundry lists lies through the relation between holism and holistic processes. Anthropology does not seek holistic perspectives as an end in itself. Rather, anthropologists use that perspective because it has been found to be crucial for solving some of the major riddles of human existence. In broadest terms, these riddles have to do with the following:

- The origins and spread of the hominids.
- The origins and spread of *Homo sapiens*.
- The causes and effects of human biological polymorphisms.
- The origin of human linguistic capacity and the origin and spread of human languages.
- The emergence of human consciousness; the origin of human society and culture.
- The causes of the divergent and convergent evolution of specific human societies and cultures.

In addition to its concern with the grand theory of human and cultural evolution, and its open-ended multidisciplinary scope, processual holism implies a commitment to a definite set of epistemological and methodological options:

Mental/Behavioral

Activity, defined as body-part motions with environmental effects, as well as thoughts, or internal cognitive events, are domains encompassed by the data sets of processual holism. Anthropological paradigms that opt for restricting the field of cultural studies to mental events (e.g., Robarchek

1989; Geertz 1973) fall outside of all definitions of holism, not merely outside of the definition of processual holism.

Emic/Etic

Both stances are requisite to processual holism. Given the current ascendancy of paradigms that define culture in purely mental and emic terms, it seems likely that the commitment to processual holism is in decline. Paradigms that confine culture to emic and mental components cannot be regarded as holistic.

Globally Comparative

Processual holism requires the use of the comparative method to test causal hypotheses about general processes. Samples drawn from global databases such as the Human Relations Area Files are a regular feature of the development of globally-applicable holistic theory.

Diachronic/Synchronic

Processes unfold through time, giving rise to convergent and divergent biocultural and sociocultural systems. The latter can therefore be viewed in a slice-of-time, as well as a developmental, perspective. Processual holism requires the use of both diachronic and synchronic methods. In the synchronic mode we have ethnography, human biology, medical anthropology, and descriptive linguistics; while in the diachronic mode we encounter archaeology and prehistory, history, paleodemography, paleontology, historical linguistics, and many other time-oriented approaches.

~

Much of the appeal of anthropology to its practitioners and students formerly derived from the traditional image of anthropology as a holistic discipline. As we have seen, however, what the textbooks and the teachers mean by holism is not necessarily holistic, nor is it distinctive of anthropology. In fact, some constructions of holism deliberately exclude major aspects of anthropological knowledge (such as the four fields or etics). Processual holism is more inclusive than the alternatives and certainly has never been popular outside of anthropology. It remains to be seen, however, if anthropologists are ready to broaden their commitment to the methods and goals of truly holistic paradigms.

Anthropologists who are committed to holism must come to terms with the risks of making mistakes. In this connection, warning students that the findings of science are provisional and subject to various distortions and biases may help to relieve some of the angst associated with holistic perspectives. Another point to be kept in mind is that the misinformation transmitted through a holistic text or introductory class is not likely to be as remote from current expert opinion as the usual non-academic sources of knowledge about biocultural evolution, such as creationism and New Age necromancy. Bear in mind that only a very small percentage of students take introductory courses in anthropology in order to prepare for graduate school; the great majority are only passing through, and one anthropology course is all they will ever take. Indeed, that one anthropology course may be the only course in the social sciences they will ever take. Given the facts that anthropology has so much to say, that its knowledge is vital for our ability to live as informed and responsible citizens of the world, and that there is so little time and space in which to say it, our students deserve to have us try to give them the most holistic view possible.

Chapter 11

Cultural Materialism

Cultural materialism (CM) is a processually holistic and globally comparative scientific research strategy. It is concerned with diachronic and synchronic, long term and short term, emic and etic, and behavioral and semiotic phenomena. In addition, it prioritizes material, behavioral, and etic conditions and processes in the explanation of the divergent, convergent, and parallel evolution of human sociocultural systems (Harris 1968, 1979; Margolis and Murphy 1995).

MATERIALISM

The materialism of cultural materialism is concerned with the locus of causality in sociocultural systems, and not with the ontological question of whether the essence of being is idea (spirit) or matter. The central issue is whether the main force of sociocultural selection emanates from infrastructure or from some other sector of the system. By infrastructure is meant the etic behavioral modes of production and reproduction as constituted by a conjunction of demographic, economic, technological, and environmental variables. Two other major universal sectors, or subsystems, complete the systemic configuration: structure, consisting of the organizational features that constitute domestic and political economy; and the symbolic and ideational sector, or "superstructure."

Economics

Ambiguities about the meaning of economics need to be resolved. Economics appears as a component of both the infrastructural and structural subsystems. In the infrastructure, economics denotes the predominant production practices, such as foraging, irrigation agriculture, or industrial factory production—the mode of subsistence, in other words. In the structure, economics denotes the manner in which economic effort is organized. The latter corresponds to the Marxist notion of the social relations of production—relations governed by such institutions as private or communal property and wages or other forms of compensation and exchange. Industrial factories, for example, are an infrastructural feature, while the organization of the factory—whether by worker's committees or by elite managers—is a structural feature.

In conformity with the principle of the primacy of infrastructure, cultural materialism proposes to explain the variations and evolution of sociocultural systems, including domestic and political economies, in terms of a system's infrastructural features. This differs from Marxist formulations, which locate relations of production in the base and which therefore tend to view them as material conditions that act upon infrastructure as much as they are acted upon.

The Primacy of Infrastructure

The basic theoretical principle of cultural materialism has been called the "principle of infrastructural determinism," but the appellation "primacy of infrastructure" seems a more appropriate phrase in view of the widespread misunderstanding of the relationship between human agency and the determinism that prevails in sociocultural evolution, and which is discussed later in this chapter. The principle of the primacy of infrastructure holds that innovations that arise in the infrastructural sector are likely to be preserved and propagated if they enhance the efficiency of the productive and reproductive processes that sustain health and well-being and that satisfy basic human biopsychological needs and drives.

Innovations that are adaptive (i.e., that increase the efficiency of production and reproduction), are likely to be selected for, even if there is a marked incompatibility (contradiction) between them and preexisting aspects of the structural and symbolic-ideational sectors. Moreover, the resolution of any deep incompatibility between an adaptive infrastructural innovation and the preexisting features of the other sectors will predictably consist of substantial changes in those other sectors. In contrast, innovations of a structural or symbolic-ideational nature are likely to be selected against if there is any deep incompatibility between them and the infrastructure—that is to say, if they reduce the efficiency of the productive and reproductive processes that sustain health and well-being and that satisfy basic human biopsychological needs and drives.

A logical entailment of the principle of the primacy of infrastructure is that, given similar evolved infrastructural complexes in different societies, one can expect convergence toward similar structural relationships and symbolic-ideational features. The reverse also holds: different infrastructures lead to different structures and different symbols and ideas.

WHO BENEFITS?

I hasten to emphasize that the costs and benefits of innovations may refer to the health and well-being of an entire population or to groups, some of which may have separate and conflicting interests in the consequences of particular innovations. This proviso corrects the common misunderstanding that cultural materialism is a "Panglossian" form of functionalism. In the presence of groups with conflicting interests, selection for or against innovations depends on the relative power that each group can exert on behalf of its own interests. Unlike most Marxian treatments of this problem, however, cultural materialism recognizes the occurrence of innovations that simultaneously benefit both subordinate and superordinate groups. In stratified societies, substantial changes in any sector generally occur only when they benefit the superordinate groups (classes, genders, ethnicities) to some extent; but this does not mean that the subordinate groups do not benefit, if generally to a lesser degree, from the same innovations.

The evolution of preindustrial states provides a convenient example: commoners benefitted from the agro-managerial functions of the ruling elites, but the ruling elites benefitted far more from their imposition of tributary labor and other forms of taxation. Similarly, women in the United States have benefitted from their integration into the wage labor market; their employers have gained even more from the infusion of cheap labor into the work force.

CAUSALITY

Because of its functionalist affinities, cultural materialism has often been pictured as involving a teleological form of causality in which the system seems to know beforehand which way it is going and in which effects seem to precede causes. It is important, therefore, to point out that the causality embraced by cultural materialism corresponds to what B. F. Skinner (1984) called "selection by consequences." Innovations in cultural repertories arise from many sources (some conscious, others unconscious) and are continuously subjected to tests of their contribution to health and well being. Some are selected for and propagated across the generations; others are selected against and eliminated. As in natural selection and operant conditioning, neither cultural materialism's system nor the actors necessarily know where they are going. Sociocultural selection, like other instances of selection by consequences, is largely opportunistic and devoid of mysterious teleological forces.

CONVERGENT AND PARALLEL EVOLUTION

Massive amounts of empirical findings support cultural materialism's claim that sociocultural evolution can be understood in terms of nomothetic processes. Despite the currently fashionable postmodernist premise that cultural differences and similarities are inappropriate candidates for scientific explanations, ethnographic, historical, and archaeological data indicate that human sociocultural systems have undergone a high degree of parallel and convergent evolution. Parallels and convergences in the evolution of New World and Old World political economies are difficult to dismiss as quirky stochastic effects (e.g., the independently evolved complexes surrounding ruling elites, use of preciosities consisting of rare metals and minerals, pyramids with hidden burial chambers, brother-sister marriage, human sacrifice, god-kings, astronomy, solar and lunar calendars, mathematics, etc.). Similarly, hundreds of studies based on the Human Relations Area Files or other large-scale comparative databases clearly demonstrate the nonrandom nature of sociocultural selection.

NEUTRAL AND DYSFUNCTIONAL FEATURES

This is not to say that all infrastructural, structural, and symbolic-ideational features are explicable in terms of infrastructural cost-benefit reckonings. There are many instances in which innovations are adaptively neutral. Take, for example, the customary colors of clothing given as gifts to babies in the United States: pink for girls and blue for boys. This color code might originally have been selected for because of the association of blue with royalty and male prerogatives, which was linked to the difficulty of obtaining blue dyes. In modern contexts, however, blue for boys and pink for girls seems to be selectively neutral—that is, blue could mean girl and pink could mean boy without any serious consequences. What might continue to be adaptively important, however, is the use of colors that, like blue and pink, lie at opposite ends of the visible spectrum.

Many other traits may be adaptively significant yet completely arbitrary within a set of functionally equivalent alternatives. There is more than one way to shape an effective projectile, fashion a serviceable pot, design a computer program, or, in the vernacular, "skin a cat."

Finally, other traits may be maladaptive, or "dysfunctional," in the sense that they diminish rather than enhance the health and well-being of an entire population. Robert Edgerton (1992), in his book, *Sick Societies*, argues that cultural materialists and cultural ecologists have grossly

exaggerated the extent to which various beliefs and practices make positive contributions to health and well-being. Witchcraft accusations, witch
hunts, revenge feuding, male supremacy, and self-imposed nutritional
deficits are some of the traits that Edgerton regards as dysfunctional. In
rebuttal, I would emphasize again (as in the Who Benefits? section above)
the need to distinguish between cost-benefits that accrue equally to all
segments, genders, classes, etc., and cost-benefits that accrue unequally,
placing some groups in the position of being dominated and exploited by
others, as in the case of slavery or colonialism. Slavery and colonialism are
clearly dysfunctional arrangements for the dominated groups, but not
necessarily for the slave owners and colonialists.

Truly maladaptive or dysfunctional traits are beliefs and activities
from which no one gains and everyone loses. Examples come readily to
mind in the form of suicide cults, such as that in Jonestown, Guyana, where
nine hundred cult members drank Kool-Aid laced with poison and died,
or the thirty-nine men and women who killed themselves at Rancho
Santa Fe, California, in 1997, in expectation of boarding spaceships to
another world.

Far from denying the occurrence of maladaptive-dysfunctional traits,
cultural materialism envisions such traits as an inevitable accompaniment
of the processes of cultural evolution. Selection by consequence means
that innovations are continuously subject to being selected for or against
in conformity with their contribution to health and well-being. It would
be surprising if there was never an innovation that had negative consequences for everybody. On the other hand, one doesn't expect sociocultural systems to consist in large measure of maladaptive-dysfunctional
traits—to be truly sick in Edgerton's sense—if selection by consequences
is continuously operative. Sick societies either change or die.

Contrary to Edgerton's claim, if anthropologists have exaggerated
anything, it is the belief that cultures consist of heavy doses of dysfunctional traits. The Boasians, especially Robert Lowie (1920), delighted in
identifying quirky and antieconomic ethnographic features, such as the
Chinese rejection of milk for aesthetic reasons; the failure of the Shilluk,
Zulu, and other African groups to use their cattle for meat except on fes-

tive occasions; and the great attention paid by such peoples to twisting the horns of their cattle into "grotesque shapes" that lacked economic utility. Lowie's other prize examples are the horses eaten but not milked in Western Europe, pigs raised in Egypt "with not one practical purpose," and Aborigines in Australia keeping the dingo as a pet "without training it to catch game or render any service whatsoever." Given these pronouncements, the challenge confronting anthropology is to formulate explanations of these and similar apparently quirky and useless cultural phenomena (e.g., food preferences and avoidances [Harris 1985]).

Thus, cultural materialism does not deny that there are neutral and dysfunctional as well as functional traits. It does maintain, however, that such features cannot be identified *a priori* and that therefore claims for their existence must be subjected to rigorous scrutiny accompanied by the testing of alternative theories.

THE ROLE OF MEANING AND IDEAS

A common misrepresentation of cultural materialism is that it either ignores the symbolic, semiotic, and ideational aspects of human social life or reduces them to mere epiphenomena. This assessment ignores the emphasis of cultural materialism on sociocultural *systems*. The latter are systems by virtue of the complex feedbacks and interactions between all the major components. As systems, they can no more dispense with their symbolic-ideational components than they can dispense with their infrastructural components. What the principle of the primacy of infrastructure asserts is not that infrastructure is the most indispensable part of the system, but that infrastructure is the most important locus of selection for and against sociocultural innovations.

Moreover, the primacy of infrastructure does not mean that, during the course of sociocultural evolution, symbolic-ideational factors are always the passive recipients of impulses originating in the infrastructure. Symbolic-ideational configurations are not necessarily Marx's cheap opiate. Rather, they often are stimulants that energize and mobilize people

and resources on behalf of particular kinds of sociocultural change. They
do so successfully, however, only to the extent that they feed back to and
are compatible with evolving infrastructural conditions.

RELIGION IN COMMAND?

The direction of causality in cultural evolution can often be obscured if
one observes the feedback between the symbolic-ideational, structural,
and infrastructural components only in the short run. For example, if we
observe the recent process of change in Iran starting with the overthrow of
the Shah, we seem to be in the presence of a wholesale refutation of the
primacy of infrastructure. One might claim that "religion is in command"
since it is the Islamic revitalization that toppled the Shah and brought the
Mullahs to power. But the systemic sources of these events are not to be
found in the Islamic ideology the Ayatollah Khomeini brought to Iran
from his exile in France. One must step back to the despotic and exploitative colonial infrastructure that had been imposed upon Iran in the aftermath of World War II, and to the struggle against the attempt of Western
oil companies to gain control of Iran's oil reserves.

Similarly, the future of Iran's Islamic Republic will not be settled by
the fundamentalism of the Mullahs, but by the secularizing trends of industrialization and the price of oil.

POLITICS IN COMMAND?

The recent history of China invites a comparable analysis concerning relations between structural (political-economic) configurations and infrastructure. Under the auspices of Mao Tse Tung, China during the 1960s
and 1970s pursued a policy of "politics in command." This involved abandoning the use of material rewards as an incentive for modernizing China's
mode of production. Politics in command licensed the Red Guards to ter-

rorize the labor force, but production fell and millions died in famines that the government tried to conceal. Politics in command was selected against in favor of a mixture of consumer capitalism and an authoritarian state. It was selected against because it proved to be incompatible with rapid industrialization, or in classic Marxist terms, it proved to be a "fetter" on the development of the forces of production. In retrospect we see that politics were in command for only a brief interval.

A similar analysis can be made of the collapse of Soviet and East European authoritarian-state socialist regimes. For a decade or so after World War II, these regimes experienced high rates of industrialization and rapidly rising standards of living. By the 1970s, however, standards of living leveled off or began to decline. The stage was set for the transition from smokestack forms of industrialism to the high-tech microelectronic industrialism that already had become established in the West. The ossified bureaucracy that ran the Soviet economy, however, restrained the expansion and transformation of the Soviet infrastructure. Amid mounting corruption and inefficiency, the old political economy of state socialism was selected against. What will take its place as yet remains obscure, but there is no reason to believe that the dominant selection process has shifted to the structural or symbolic-ideational sectors of Soviet society.

LONG AND SHORT TERM

Some anthropologists accept the principle of the primacy of infrastructure when applied to long-term events, such as the origin of states or the rise of nonkilling religions. Such events involve time measured in centuries, or "even millennia." But according to R. Brian Ferguson (1995:30), "in dealing with time frames measured in decades, years, and even shorter spans, cultural materialist theory is weak." The concern here is that if cultural materialism is only appropriate for understanding long-term changes, it cannot be important for policy-making with respect to vital current interests. It is by no means clear, however, that cultural materialism cannot deal with events unfolding over decades, as the two examples cited above indicate. When we get down to years and days, the penumbras of uncertainty necessarily grow larger.

At some point, Ferguson suggests, we would do better to adopt a purely historical (idiographic) stance. In rebuttal, however, I would argue that cultural materialism remains relevant to some (even if not all) unfolding events in the short term of years and days. Consider, for example, the enormous changes that are taking place day by day in the economic organization, work patterns, and ideology as the industrial infrastructure converts to the use of computers. The principle of the primacy of infrastructure may not be able to explain all of the details of these changes, but it can explain a great deal of what is happening before our eyes.

HUMAN AGENCY

Another point that needs clarification is the role of human agency in the explanation of sociocultural differences and similarities. The greatest barrier to the acceptance of determinist views of history is the misapprehension that they rob human beings of any motivation for social and political activism. On the contrary, in the perspective of cultural materialism, selection for or against an innovation is carried out by individuals who respond to the cost-benefit balance associated with alternative means of satisfying their basic biopsychological needs and drives. The aggregate vectors of these decisions and their enactment in behavior add up to the preservation or extinction of old or new patterns.

If this process results in predictable or retrodictable patterns of thought and behavior, it is not because a mysterious teleological supraindividual force or system has imposed its will on individuals, but because individuals who are confronted with similar constraints and opportunities tend to make similar choices regarding their self-interest. The freedom of human agents, as manifested in their ability to negotiate a better deal for themselves, is not enhanced by denying the deterministic aspects of social life. Rather, the enhancement of freedom depends in large measure on the conscious examination of the material constraints and opportunities, costs as well as benefits, in the long as well as the short run. If social life were as chaotic as many postmodernists and idealists allege, there could be no rational choice, nor anyone to negotiate with. The enemy of human agency is not historical determinism but the frivolous conceit that humans are free to shape the social world in any direction they please.

PROBABILISTIC DETERMINISM

The determinism embraced by cultural materialism has little to do with the determinism of nineteenth-century mechanical systems. As we have just seen, theories of sociocultural evolution must contend with a loose fit between individual preferences and calculations of self-interest; while on a higher level of abstraction, as indicated previously, items selected for or against may differ because they are functionally neutral or functionally equivalent. Finally, also as indicated, the causality of cultural materialism is not that of billiard balls but of "selection by consequence." For these reasons, cultural materialism embraces a form of determinism best described as probabilistic. Despite this qualification, a world of difference separates cultural materialism from the ascendant idiographic and interpretive paradigms of the last quarter of the twentieth century that have abandoned the effort to push the scientific study of the causality that operates in human sociocultural systems to their outer limits.

While insisting that determinate causal processes operate in history, and that human will and consciousness are dominated by infrastructural conditions, cultural materialism claims to be compatible with conscious attempts by individuals to control their own destinies and to construct a progressive social order. The opening for this volitional ingredient is provided by the probabilistic character of the determinism, as discussed above. If the influence of consciousness on history thus far has been negligible, it is not because of an implacable determinism, but because of our failure to understand the causes of sociocultural evolution and to consciously and intelligently optimize our welfare in the light of that understanding.

VALUES AND PRAXIS

Cultural materialism, unlike Marxism, does not provide a program for building a specific form of society nor propose a unity of theory and practice in bringing about a specific utopian outcome (e.g., the destruction of capitalism). Yet cultural materialism's epistemological and theoretical principles may in themselves be counted as a challenge to the status quo and as a contribution to progressive change since they call into question established wisdom concerning the relationship between ideas and behavior, thereby raising consciousness to new levels of awareness.

Chapter 12

Postmodernism

WHAT IS POSTMODERNISM?

Postmodernism (Pomo) is an intellectual movement or orientation that promotes itself as the antithesis of modernism. The term itself was introduced by architects in the late 1940s. While the themes of postmodernism actually originated long before anyone started to design postmodern buildings—with their celebration of anything-goes stylistic juxtapositions and avoidance of repetitive glass-box effects—current architectural trends have some marginal illustrative utility. Postmodernism, however, is a much more complex phenomenon than just an architectural extravaganza.

Of the many intellectual strands that run through postmodernism, the most prominent and important is the disparagement of Western science and technology. Other strands that follow from this central tenet include:

- The representation of social life as a "text."
- The elevation of text and language as the fundamental phenomena of existence.
- The application of literary analysis to all phenomena.
- The questioning of reality and of the adequacy of language to describe reality.
- Disdain for, or rejection of, method.
- Rejection of broad theories or metanarratives.
- Advocacy of polyvocality.

- Focus on power relations and cultural hegemony.
- Rejection of Western institutions and achievements.
- Extreme relativism and a tendency toward nihilism. (Adapted from Kuznar 1997)

To postmodernists, science is an ideological product embedded in a particular cultural context. There is little that is new in this proposal given the long-standing appeal of the sociology of knowledge (Mannheim 1936), the broad Marxist and cultural materialist models of the relationship between base and superstructure (Blackburn 1972), and the long-standing debate about "value-free" social science. Much has been written, for example, about the influence of classical laissez-faire capitalism on Darwin's view of "struggle for survival"(e.g., Hofstadter 1955). Another example is the influence of the observer's class and race on attempts to provide objective measurements of intelligence (Kamin 1974). In my own case, I have no difficulty whatsoever with the postmodernist discovery that science is culturally embedded and culturally constructed, since I have long characterized science as a form of ideology (but a very distinctive one—*sui generis*).

In its stronger versions, however, postmodernists go far beyond recognition of observer bias in the framing and conduct of scientific inquiry. Unlike Marx and Engels (and other critics of positivism), the leading figures in postmodernism, such as Jean-Francois Lyotard, Paul DeMan, Jacques Derrida, and Michel Foucault (in concert, if not individually), attack the entire scientific enterprise, including its empirical, logical, and ethical-moral foundations.

For postmodernists there are no privileged paradigms. Science gets no closer to truth than any other "reading" of an unknowable and undecidable world. "Nothing can be proved, nothing can be falsified." (Ferry and Renaut 1988, quoted in Rosenau 1992:134). Truth is "persuasive fiction." More ominously, according to Michel Foucault, knowledge is the discourse of power:

> There is no power relation without the correlative
> constitution of a field of knowledge, nor any knowledge
> that does not presuppose and constitute at the same time
> power relations. (1984:175)

Foucault's concern is not that science is incapable of finding truth, but that science is dehumanizing. Nonetheless, his basic idea, that a mode of discourse is inevitably a code of power relations among the people who use it,

> has contributed importantly to the notion that science is
> simply a cultural construct, which in both form and
> content, and independently of any individual scientist's
> wish, is deeply inscribed with assumptions about
> domination, mastery, and authority. (Gross and Levitt
> 1994:78)

Thus, postmodernists associate science and reason with the domination and oppression of totalitarian regimes. Since science searches for a "best answer," it precludes diversity and leads to intolerance. In postmodern eyes, "reasonable" ways are always brutally unfair to somebody. Modernists, they claim, merely use science and reason to legitimate their preconceptions. In her book, *Post-Modernism and the Social Sciences*, Pauline Rosenau explains that abandoning reason

> means for post-modernists, liberation from modernity's
> preoccupation with authority, efficiency, hierarchy, power,
> technology, commerce (the business ethic), adminis-
> tration, social engineering. . . . It means release from
> modern science's concern for order, consistency, predict-
> ability . . . . (1992:129)

And, at still greater remove, postmodernists seek to replace science and reason with emotion, feeling, introspection, intuition, autonomy, creativity, imagination, fantasy, and contemplation (ibid.). They favor the heart over the head, the spiritual over the mechanical, the personal over the impersonal.

Postmodernists reject broad generalizations and so-called "totalizing" theories. Truth, in addition to being persuasive fiction, is relative, local, plural, indefinite, and interpretive. Thus the attempt to provide objective ethnographic data must be abandoned. In the words of Marilyn Strathern,

> The observer/observed relationship can no longer be
> assimilated to that between subject and object. The
> object(ive) is a joint production. Many voices, multiple
> texts, plural authorship. (1987:264–5)

The former self-authorizing text by which the returning field worker spoke for another society in a "determining way ... now appears repugnant" (ibid.).

POMO MODES OF DISCOURSE

Everything wrong with society is no longer to be explained by the mode of production, but rather by the mode of discourse; and the production of knowledge is seen as more important than the production of goods or services. Could there be a theory better suited for the approbation of the part of the labor force that makes its living from selling words?

Under postmodern auspices, subjectivism, relativism, particularism, and nihilism have become ascendant themes among anthropologists (and other sociocultural "disciplines" [Collins 1989]). In conformity with their commitment to a disjointed, collage-like view of the human condition, many postmodernists have achieved the ability to write about their thoughts in a uniquely impenetrable manner. Their neobaroque prose style—with its inner clauses, bracketed syllables, metaphors and metonyms, verbal pirouettes, curlicues and filigrees—is not a mere epiphenomenon; rather, it is a mocking rejoinder to anyone who would try to write simple intelligible sentences in the modernist tradition.

I give you here, for example, an epistle from Clifford Geertz, the reluctant father of postmodern interpretive anthropology, whilst he ruminated on the fact that cultures are collages, in a book that purports to inform graduate students about trends in cultural anthropology:

> Our response to this, so it seems to me, commanding fact,
> is, so it also seems to me, one of the major moral
> challenges we these days face, ingredient in virtually all
> others we face, from nuclear disarmament to the equitable
> distribution of the world's resources, and in facing it
> counsels of indiscriminate tolerance, which are any way
> not genuinely meant, and my target here, of surrender,
> proud, cheerful, defensive, or resigned, to the pleasures of
> invidious comparison serve us equally badly; though the
> latter is perhaps the more dangerous because the more
> likely to be followed. (1994:465)

POSTPROCESSUALISM

One of the most influential expressions of postmodernism in anthropology is the archaeological movement that calls itself postprocessualism. As summed up by Richard Watson, postprocessualists

> use deconstructionist skeptical arguments to conclude that
> there is no objective past and that our representations of
> the past are only texts that we produce on the basis of our
> socio-political standpoints. In effect they argue that there
> is no objective world, that the world itself is a text that
> human beings produce. (1990:673)

Ian Hodder, of Cambridge University, is the leading postprocessual archaeologist. He claims modern generalizing and evolutionary archaeology are defective because they fail to deal with "the meaningful construction of social acts and the historical particularity of human culture" (Hodder 1985:22). For Hodder, recognition of the meaningful component in social acts precludes explanations that incorporate factors external to human agency:

> cultures . . . are arbitrary in the sense that their forms and
> content are not determined by anything outside of
> themselves. . . . Culture then is not reducible, it just is.
> (1986:2)

The reason that scientists favor knowledge produced in conformity with the epistemological principles of science is not because science guarantees absolute truth free of subjective bias, error, untruths, lies, and frauds, but because science is the best system yet devised for reducing subjective bias, error, untruths, lies, and frauds.

IMPROVING THE RELIABILITY OF ETHNOGRAPHY

Science-minded anthropologists seek to obtain reliable data as gauged by the ability of independent observers to replicate each other's findings. But postmodernists are quick to point out that there is little in the ethnographic literature that has been replicated by a second observer. Ethnographers have almost always worked alone; therefore, postmodernists claim, ethnographic objectivity is a fiction (Marcus and Fischer 1986; Sanjek 1990:394).

The admittedly shallow forms of reliability in the ethnographic literature, however, deserve a wholly different programmatic interpretation. I am not aware that anyone has shown that the reliability of ethnographic descriptions cannot be improved because there is some fatal warp in the universe that precludes two or more ethnographers from employing similar research protocols or from working at the same time in the same community. There are certainly plenty of centrally planned ethnographic undertakings in which teams of ethnographers have worked together, although their final reports or dissertations only rarely been have issued as team products. Clearly, this whole argument arises from circumstances completely extraneous to the epistemological disputations of postmodernism. The limited reliability of ethnographic accounts is an aspect of the pauperization of the social sciences in combination with the highly individualized system of academic rewards that prevails almost everywhere.

Human Agency

As previously noted, the greatest barrier to the acceptance of scientific determinist views of history is the misapprehension that they rob human beings of any motivation for social and political activism. A peculiar terror seems to grip postmodernists at the mere mention of the word *cause*. It is as if by the mere act of speaking about the causes of sociocultural evolution, one can deliver our species to the totalizing bondage of evil theories.

~

My defense of science and objectivity is not intended to be a cover-up for the failure of science and technology on their own to improve the fundamental quality of human life. If I had to name the century now drawing to a close, I would call it "The Century of Broken Dreams." It has not made the world safe for democracy, banished war, ended poverty, abolished exploitation, or raised everybody's standard of living. Furthermore, much of our disappointment derives directly from the unintended and unforeseen consequences of science and technology, such as environmental pollution or computer-driven bureaucracies (Harris 1989:495ff). But it would be a grave error to conclude that, by withdrawing support from science and technology at the beginning of the century, the end would have been more satisfactory.

Until it is shown that the costs of science necessarily outweigh its benefits, the solution to bad science is better science (Reyna 1994; D'Andrade 1995; Harris 1995). This is especially clear in the case of unintended consequences that are avoidable and remediable by improving and enlarging the anthropological science component in the assessment of the effects of technological change.

Part IV

Macroevolution

Chapter 13

Origins of Capitalism

A perennial problem addressed by scholars interested in the macroprocesses of sociocultural evolution is why capitalism developed first in Europe and why it developed between the fourteenth and sixteenth centuries. Stephen Sanderson (1994) has recently reviewed the standard explanations, exposed their faults, and offered his own theory to explain the origins of capitalism.

Sanderson suggests that since capitalism developed independently in Japan not long after it developed in Europe, any nomothetic theory of the origins of capitalism must be able to explain both cases. Although I am in thorough agreement with this contention, it is important to bear in mind that there were specific differences between Japanese and European feudalism that are relevant to the origins of capitalism, and that these also need to be explained. In this chapter I examine Sanderson's theory from a cultural-materialist perspective and propose an alternative theory that explains both the origins of feudalism and capitalism and their variations in terms of the principle of the primacy of infrastructure.

CAPITALISM DEFINED

The question of capitalism's origins in Europe and Japan presumes, of course, that the conjunction of infrastructural, structural, and symbolic-ideational features that appeared in Europe between the fifteenth and sixteenth centuries, and about two centuries later in Japan, represented something radically different from all preceding sociocultural genera. These distinctive features include:

- The pervasive commodification of virtually all goods and services, including land and labor.
- Trading in stocks and bonds.
- The relentless pursuit of profits by individuals and firms in virtually every instance of production, distribution, and consumption.
- The accumulation of profits to form capital.
- The reinvestment of capital to make more profits and more capital, and the enforcement of economic contracts by courts and governments.

To be sure, elements of this system were present in various non-European societies long before the fifteenth century. Markets, money, merchants, contracts, private property, and production for profit were present in Sumer and Babylon, Pharaonic Egypt, Han China, and Gangetic India, as well as in ancient Greece and Rome. In all such instances, however, the capitalist elements were subordinate to other political-economic structures. In Mesopotamia, Egypt, Gangetic India, and ancient China, the agro-managerial functions of the state were the principal source of wealth and power. Merchants flourished at the pleasure of the supreme rulers and their agro-managerial bureaucracies. The state established monopolies over the most lucrative trade items, mines, and industries. Moreover, none of these societies possessed well-developed wage labor markets. The basic tasks of subsistence fell on the backs of peasant farmers, who were constrained by various forms of peonage, serfdom, slavery, and clientage to remain immobilized in their ancestor's villages.

There were also many elements of capitalism present within ancient Europe, especially in the city-states of Greece and republican Rome. Trade in wine and grains was essential for the subsistence of these urbanized societies and provided the basis for the rise of a powerful merchant class; but the task of producing these commodities increasingly depended on the work of slaves rather than on wage laborers. Out of a population of 270,000 in fifth-century Athens, 80,000 to 100,000 were slaves (Stearns et al. 1992:135). Italy in A.D. 14 had three million slaves—40 percent of the total population. Although slaves as persons could be bought and sold, and thus were to a certain extent commodified, they were not allowed to sell their own labor without their owner's permission. Slavery in ancient Greece and Rome thus ran directly against one of the defining conditions of capitalism, the compensation for labor by means of wages.

Max Weber's Theory

Max Weber proposed the prevailing explanation for why capitalism arose in Europe. Firmly in the idealist camp, Weber ([1904]1958) linked capitalism to the Protestant Reformation. According to Weber, Protestantism supported values that favored the accumulation of capital: thrift, hard work, and material and spiritual salvation by means of individual effort. Granting that he never proposed that religion was the sole cause of capitalism, the lingering popularity accorded Weber's approach is ill-deserved. Even within Europe, the rise of capitalism was not confined to the Protestant states. Catholic Venice, for example, was one of the most precocious centers of capitalist development. And as Sanderson points out, the existence of an independent parallel transition from feudalism to capitalism in Japan—a fact of which Weber was unaware—contradicts the essence of his theory. For Weber, it was the contemplative and ascetic slant of Far Eastern religions that accounted for a supposedly delayed movement toward capitalism in Japan.

From a cultural-materialist perspective, the resolution of this seemingly paradoxical combination of contemplative religion and capitalist drive is that, in general, the symbolic and expressive components of sociocultural systems adapt to infrastructure and political economy. In both Europe and Japan, earlier religious constructions adapted to feudalism were readily bent into forms adapted to the emergent capitalist order.

Marxist Explanations

Marxist explanations of the rise of capitalism (e.g., Dobb 1966) attributed the breakup of European feudalism to material conditions but emphasized structural features such as class conflict between peasants and feudal lords; to escape increasingly intense exploitation, for example, peasants fled to the cities and became available for wage labor. But this account does not explain why in the absence of the commodification of land and labor, class relations became exploitative to the point of self-destruction.

Sanderson's own theory is based on five basic characteristics of Europe and Japan that operated as important preconditions facilitating their transition from a feudal to a capitalist economy. The five preconditions are: demography, size, geography, climate, and political structure.

Demography

Several theories of the origin of capitalism invoke demographic factors; but as Sanderson points out, the existing demographic theories appear to take contradictory positions. Some claim that, as a result of the black death, which killed off as many as one half of Europe's population between 1350 and 1450, there was a shortage of peasant labor and that it was this shortage, more than any other factor, that undermined the foundations of feudal relationships. Others, myself included, see population pressure as one of the most important causes of the black death, the turmoil of the ensuing century, and the collapse of the manorial mode of production (Harris and Ross 1987).

Population pressure in Europe was, in turn, part of a larger causal matrix involving the intensification of agriculture, soil and forest depletions, recourse to marginal lands, declining efficiency, and other consequences of pushing the manorial mode of production to its limits (Harris 1977). I do not find it contradictory that the initial transformation to capitalism occurred when population was declining rather than increasing. The labor shortages after 1350 merely added another set of forces to those that were corroding the old manorial system and hastening the development of wage labor, commerce, and entrepreneurship. The sudden drop in population in Europe, in other words, was not a necessary cause of the transition to capitalism.

Sanderson makes a significant contribution here by comparing the demographic histories of Europe and Japan. In both instances population grew rapidly during the feudal period, but Japan experienced nothing like the European depopulation of 1350–1450. Therefore, one may conclude that it was population pressure, not depopulation, that promoted the development of capitalism:

> a "crisis of underpopulation" that would have shifted the balance of class power away from the nobility in favor of the peasantry could not have been a causal factor in Japan's capitalist transition; that should make us doubt that the population crash of late-medieval Europe played an important role in the European transition. However, it is still possible that *over*population could have been a factor in Japan, and in the European capitalist transition as well. (1994:38)

Thus, in listing demography as one of the "important preconditions" of the break-up of feudalism, Sanderson accepts a basic ingredient of the principle of the primacy of infrastructure.

Geography

Sanderson claims that the location of both Japan and the leading capitalist countries of northwest and southern Europe on large bodies of water was important for the transition to capitalism. It allowed them to carry on maritime trade, the basis for the development of a commercial economy. This claim lacks cogency, however, because China, a capitalist laggard, shares the same sea with Japan, has an enormous coastline, and possessed the largest fleet of coastal and long-distance trade vessels in the world. One can conclude that access to maritime trade routes does not mean that such routes will be used in a fashion that promotes the development of capitalist forms of trade.

Climate

Sanderson sees the fact that Japan and Europe both had temperate climates as an important precondition. Because of its temperate climate, Japan was able to escape the process of "peripheralization" at the hands of Europeans, who came to dominate the emerging world capitalist system. Sanderson suggests that Japan was a less-appealing target for European expansion than countries in which tropical and semitropical crops could be grown.

The logic here is that unless a country could avoid colonization, it would never give rise to robust forms of capitalism. (This does not seem to apply to places like Hong Kong, Brazil, and Indonesia.) As we shall see in a moment, climate does form a part of the complex of environmental constraints and opportunities that, along with the other components of infrastructure, provide the key to our problem; but as with geography, not in the way Sanderson suggests.

Size

It is important, claims Sanderson, that Japan and the most precocious European examples of the transition to capitalism were small countries. The reason for this is that "It is costly to maintain a large state because resources are drained away that could be used more directly for economic development" (1994:39). This seems a dubious connection since, other things being equal, the larger the state, the greater the potential volume of internal and external trade. Moreover, whatever the effect of size, including it in the basic preconditions for capitalist development merely leads to a more fundamental question: why were the kingdoms of Europe and Japan so small, while other states, such as China, Mesopotamia, and Egypt, were so big?

Political Structure

Sanderson identifies the decentralized political structure of European and Japanese feudalism as the fith and final important precondition for the rise of capitalism. His reasoning is that decentralization encouraged commercial activity, whereas large centralized states developed bureaucratic classes that were indifferent or hostile to commerce:

> large bureaucratic empires stifle merchant activity because it is a threat to the tributary mode through which the state extracts surplus. (1994:41)

I agree with this observation, as far as it goes, but it is not enough merely to identify the loose, small, decentralized states of feudal Europe and Japan as structurally pre-adapted to capitalism, and the centralized agro-managerial empires of China or Egypt as antagonistic to capitalism. The heart of the issue is why small feudal states, and not big bureaucratic agro-managerial ones, developed in medieval Europe and Japan. And, equally important, why did big agro-managerial empires, rather than feudal kingdoms, come to prevail in China, Egypt, Mesopotamia, and Gangetic India? Why Sanderson can remain rather indifferent to these two key questions will become clear in a moment.

THE QUESTION OF TIMING

Thus far, I have been discussing only that part of Sanderson's theory that deals with the question of why the transition to capitalism occurred first in Japan and Europe. There remains the question of timing. According to Sanderson, capitalism could not develop until the density and extent of worldwide commerce had passed a certain threshold:

> The level of world commercialization had finally built up in the centuries after 1000 A.D. to a critical density

sufficient to trigger a massive capitalist takeoff. A
threshold of commercialization as the result of expanding
urban networks and intensive trade density had been
achieved, and this led to an explosive capitalist takeoff in
those two regions of the world, western Europe and Japan,
that were most hospitable to capitalist activity. (1994:48)

Sanderson sees this commercial buildup taking 4,500 years.

The reason for his apparent indifference to the question of the origin of feudalism now becomes clear. Feudalism merely speeded up the process of commercializing the world, but that same critical threshold of commercial activity would have eventually been reached in the agro-managerial empires.

Note well that my theory holds that *capitalism would
eventually have developed anyway* given enough time for
the further buildup of world commercialization. . . . even
if there never had been any feudal societies in the world an
explosive capitalist spurt would eventually have occurred.
It may have taken a good deal more time—possibly
another millennium or two . . . but capitalism was a force
that could not be denied; its emergence was inevitable.
(1994:49; italics in original)

Sanderson offers no reasons why the absence of feudalism would have delayed the onset of capitalism by one or two thousand years (why not ten years or ten thousand?). Since there is no evidence that agro-managerial states (or any other type of nonfeudal state) ever gave rise to capitalism, the assertion of inevitability of capitalism over a definite span of time is untestable and arbitrary. There have been only two independent transitions to capitalism, both of which emerged out of feudal states. Therefore, what the evidence legitimately allows us to infer is that feudalism was a necessary precondition of capitalism. Thus, any theory of the origin of capitalism that does not explain the origin of feudalism in processual terms is less satisfactory than one that does. Moreover, identifying the conditions under which feudalism arose necessarily involves a comparative approach that identifies the conditions under which other forms of states arose, especially the bureaucratized agro-managerial empires.

My own approach to the origins of feudalism, agro-managerial empires, and capitalism derives in large measure from the work of Karl Wittfogel (1957). I accept Wittfogel's theories only with considerable modification, but I see his emphasis upon the techno-environmental components of sociocultural systems as providing the infrastructural grounding lacking in other approaches and as consistent with the paradigmatic formulations of cultural materialism and the primacy of infrastructure. For Wittfogel, the development of loose, decentralized feudal states rested on their decentralized mode of production. In Europe, the relevant mode of production was rainfall-dependent agriculture. This contrasts with the techno-environmental conjunction that prevailed in the territories of the large, agro-managerial states, where arid climates plus major river valleys that could be used for large-scale irrigation-dependent agriculture prevailed.

The productivity of the irrigation systems of Mesopotamia, Egypt, Gangetic India, and China—what Wittfogel called hydraulic societies—was maximized by the state's construction of massive dams, canals, and other hydraulic facilities and by appropriately organized bureaus that allocated labor for the construction, maintenance, and repair of these facilities and for the allocation of the irrigation system's life-sustaining waters. Thus, the elites who controlled the waterworks controlled the political economy to an extent that was never feasible in Europe; they possessed the means for achieving total power over immense territories and populations. Where rainfall agriculture prevailed, however, production did not benefit from centralization nor was a total centralization of power feasible. As Wittfogel emphasizes, periods of European political absolutism were always contested by alternative religious, commercial, and military centers of power.

But how does Japan fit into this picture, given the fact that the basic Japanese techno-environmental conjunction was not rainfall-dependent, but irrigation-dependent agriculture?

Wittfogel was well aware of this problem (see Price 1994 for an extended discussion of Wittfogel's position). Contrary to popular impression, Wittfogel did not propose that every society that practiced irrigation fitted the pattern of hydraulic society. Irrigation, in the absence of the potential of great river-valley habitats, could readily lead to modes of production that he called hydroagriculture (cf. Sidky 1996). Japan was a hydroagricultural society, not a hydraulic society:

> Why did Japan's rice economy not depend on large and government directed water works? . . . The peculiarities of the country's water supply neither necessitated or favored substantial government-directed works. Innumerable mountain ranges compartmentalized the great Far Eastern Islands; and their broken relief encouraged a fragmented (hydroagricultural) rather than a coordinated (hydraulic) pattern of irrigation farming and flood control. . . .

> They therefore failed to establish a comprehensive managerial and acquisitive bureaucracy capable of controlling the nongovernmental forces of society as did the men of the apparatus on the Chinese mainland. (Wittfogel 1957:197–8)

Despite the apparent differences between the techno-environmental components of the Japanese and European late-feudal infrastructures, basic similarities in their techno-environmental equations should be noted. In the late-feudal period, European agricultural production benefitted from a series of technological advances, such as wheeled plows, improved carts, greater deployment of horses, improved rotation of crops, water mills and wind mills, and greater availability of iron tools. All of this interacted with the upward trend in population size, population density and urbanization.

Similarly, in late-feudal Japan, innovations such as seed selection, development of new varieties of rice, leveling of paddy fields, double cropping, introduction of new threshing tools, and commercial fertilizer accompanied and interacted with the rise in population. (Smith 1966:92ff) Thus late-feudal Japan and Europe both possessed highly productive and evolving forms of agriculture capable of sustaining very rapidly growing and dense populations. This provides us with an insight concerning the limited prospect for the development of capitalism in the vast majority of other feudal states. In much of Africa south of the Sahara, for example, feudal states were based on rainfall agriculture practiced without benefit of either plows or draught animals.

Since there are substantial differences in the Japanese and European nature-culture equations, as well as in other infrastructural features, one scarcely expects there to be complete uniformity in the feudal forms that rose on their base. As characterized by Wittfogel, in both cases there existed alongside and below the sovereign, numerous lords or vassals who were politically, economically, and militarily semi-independent and who rendered only limited and conditional services to the local monarch (1957:417).

In Japan, as in Europe, there was no census, national corvée, or national road system; and Japanese feudal armies consisted of small independent bands of aristocratic warriors who fought on behalf of the landlord class as individual knights rather than as a coordinated army (1957:199). But generally speaking, Japanese feudal relationships were tighter and more ritualized, and they lay great stress on group loyalties (Stearns et al. 1992:434). There were probably fewer competing kingdoms, and overall Japan's feudalism was less decentralized than Europe's. (As many as one thousand separate polities may have existed in Europe in the fourteenth century [Jones 1987: 106]; while there were some 250 fiefs in Japan in the mid-nineteenth century [Smith 1966:202].)

According to Wittfogel, the independent church and the free guild cities of Europe had no parallel in Japan (1957:417). These differences are understandable in the light of Japan's hydroagricultural infrastructure. While the terrain inhibited the development of full-scale hydraulic institutions, the practice of hydroagriculture did call for a greater degree of centralized management than Europe's rainfall regimens.

These differences are relevant for one aspect of the question of timing in the development of capitalism. The temporal priority of European capitalism is consistent with the looser and more decentralized form of feudalism in Europe.

There remains the question of why the transition occurred when it did in terms of global patterns. Rather than assert that the density of world trade had reached a critical threshold at the end of an arbitrary 4,500 years of development, and in further conformity with the principles of cultural materialism, greater consideration should be given to demographic factors. From 1600 to 1850, Japan experienced a dramatic growth in both castle towns and major cities (Smith 1966:67).

Sanderson himself takes note of the rapid increase of population in Japan and links it to urbanization; as I have already pointed out, Europe also underwent similar rapid urbanization linked to enclosures and population pressure (despite the demographic crash of the fourteenth century). Leroy Ladurie (cited in Jones 1987:4) estimates that in France, Germany, and Britain at the start of the fourteenth century, 15 percent of the population was engaged in urban and other nonagricultural production. Thus, the timing of the expansion of world trade was linked to the technological, environmental, productive, and reproductive components of the European and Japanese infrastructures.

It should be noted that this viewpoint places world systems theories (Wallerstein 1974) in an altered perspective. It is not world trade that corroded the foundations of feudalism, but regional commerce involving the provisioning of towns and cities with food and raw materials. As noted by economic historian Eric Jones (1987:xxviii), Europe was marked by "an early rise of many-sided trade in bulk loads of everyday items. This trade stemmed from and further expanded a broader social participation in the market than was induced by luxury trades." In other words, world trade on the scale envisaged by Sanderson is better seen as a consequence of capitalism than as its cause, although of course, the two were related by positive feedback.

Chapter 14

The Soviet Collapse

Recent events in the Soviet Union are only explainable in supernatural terms.

Francis Irons, former Defense Department analyst, referring to the prophecy made by Nossa Senora de Fatima in 1917 that Russia would be converted to Catholicism (Niebuhr 1991)

You cannot put theory into your soup or Marxism into your clothes. If, after forty years of communism, a person cannot have a glass of milk or a pair of shoes, he will not believe that communism is a good thing, no matter what you tell him.

Nikita Khrushchev (quoted in Frankland 1967:149)

Within a remarkably short span of time, the political economy of the former Union of Soviet Socialist Republics underwent revolutionary changes on a scale fully equal to those of the Bolshevik revolution of 1917. The apparatus of central planning and pricing, state ownership of the means of production, subsidies and redistributive entitlements, one-party rule, and state censorship was either repudiated, eliminated, or substantially weakened and transformed. During the past decade, members of the former

---

This chapter is based on a paper delivered as the Distinguished Lecture at the ninetieth annual meeting of the American Anthropological Association, November 23, 1991, in Chicago.

Soviet Bloc have been searching frantically for ways to enlarge the sphere of profit-oriented private ownership.

This turn of events has led to a spectacle that few observers, West or East, ever expected to see in their lifetimes: Soviet leaders begging Japan and the West to buy up plants and facilities at fire-sale prices; apostate communists standing hat-in-hand outside of the International Monetary Fund or traveling from one erstwhile capitalist enemy to another to plead for emergency food donations. Equally astonishing has been the destruction of the Soviet empire, shattered not by nuclear warheads from abroad but by explosive ethnic and nationalist politics among its own peoples.

What do anthropologists have to say about all this? A branch of the human sciences that ignores these immense events, that interprets them primarily in terms of relativized "local knowledge," or that derides the attempt to understand them in terms of nomothetic principles, runs the risk of being confined to the backwaters of contemporary intellectual life. The purpose of this chapter is to discuss some of the salient theoretical and paradigmatic implications of the abrupt end of Soviet communism and Russian hegemony. Of overriding interest in this connection are the implications of these events for anthropological theory, especially for Marxism and alternative forms of materialism.

STRATEGIES FOR SAVING MARXISM

The collapse of the Soviet political economy has contributed to the widespread conviction that Marxism is dead (e.g., Hollander 1990). Few would deny that the end of Soviet-style authoritarian state communism diminishes the credibility of every government, party, or movement that identifies itself as following a Marxist program (Heilbronner 1990; Howe 1990); but for many Marxists, these actual or impending political defeats do not necessarily translate into the refutation of classical (pre-Leninist) Marxist theories of history.

For some Western Marxists, the collapse of the Soviet Bloc does not even signify a serious challenge to Leninist versions of Marxism. They blame the collapse on political incompetence rather than on systemic failure. For example, according to Victor Perlo (1991:11), chairman of the Economics Commission of the Communist Party (U.S.), the major problem is not Marxist theory but the breakdown in the unity of the Soviet Communist Party. "Indeed, without that division, the crisis could not have arisen" (Perlo 1991:17).

Other attempts to save Marxism contend in effect that the Soviet system represented a distortion of Marx's program for achieving the transition to genuine communism. For example, while Marx and Engels envisioned a "dictatorship of the proletariat" as a phase in the transition from capitalism to communism (Draper 1987:26), the dictatorship they anticipated was that of proletarians as a class ruling over their enemies, not the dictatorship of a party ruling over the proletariat. It is certainly difficult to find in the writings of Marx and Engels the idea that the transition to communism could only be achieved by a one-party dictatorship imposed on the workers. In Engels's words,

> If anything is established, it is that our party and the
> working class can come to power only under the form of
> the democratic republic. This is even the specific form for
> the dictatorship of the proletariat.

According to the Executive Committee of the Socialist Party of Great Britain,

> Something certainly has crumbled in Eastern Europe, but
> it has not been socialism, communism, or Marxism. For
> this to have happened, these would have had to exist there
> in the first place, but they did not. What did exist there
> and what has crumbled is Leninism and totalitarian state
> capitalism. (1990:5)

Similarly, one can reject the collapse of the Soviet Bloc as a test of Marxist theories on the grounds that the Russian revolution itself violated Marx's fundamental prescription for a successful transition to communism

(Kolakowski 1978). Russia, with its huge semifeudal peasantry, was the least appropriate locus for acting out Marx's revolutionary scenario. Marxists may thus argue that, from its inception, Russian "communism" was an aberration, a terrible mistake. Since its rise and its despotic nature were neither advocated nor predicted by Marx, its fall can scarcely be regarded as a refutation of Marxism.

In the words of economist Samuel Bowles, the revolutions in the former Soviet Bloc "have removed a millstone from the neck of leftist economists in the West" (quoted in Wallich and Corcoran 1991:135). This line of reasoning leads some Western Marxists to euphoric conclusions. They reason that Leninism-Stalinism was not merely a degenerate form of communism but its very negation. Its collapse therefore may allow "the authentic Marxist tradition, long driven underground, to return to the light of day" (Callinicos 1991:136). Now that the "muck" has been cleared away, real Marxism, which since the 1920s has been "persecuted and derided," can come into its own:

> Now classical Marxism can finally shake itself free of the
> Stalinist incubus and seize the opportunities offered by a
> world experiencing greater uncertainty and agitation than
> for many decades. (Callinicos 1991: 136)

In a similar mood, others see the collapse of the Soviet system as but the latest in a series of temporary setbacks that have periodically marked the history of Marxism, but from which the paradigm has always emerged with its core intact, and more compelling than ever. Michael Buraway, for example, argues that since Marxism provides a fecund understanding of capitalism's inherent contradictions and dynamics, the more capitalism flourishes throughout the world, the more Marxism will flourish with it:

> With the ascendancy of capitalism on a world scale,
> Marxism will therefore, once more, come into its own . . .
> the longevity of capitalism guarantees the longevity of
> Marxism. (Buraway 1990:791–2)

All of these attempts to insulate classical Marxist theories of history from the history of the Soviet Union have a hollow ring. Marx's most important historical theory, after all, was that capitalism was soon (certainly by the end of the twentieth century) to be replaced by communism or a system that was transitional to communism. While it is virtually certain that the political economy toward which the former members of the Soviet Bloc are evolving will not be the fictional unrestrained, unregulated, free-market system promoted by capitalist ideologues, the revolutionary changes of the past decade cannot realistically be regarded as a harbinger of communism. Indeed, in the present political milieu, the very word itself is as much of an electoral liability in the former Soviet Bloc as in the West. Thus, 1990–1991 must be added to the already extensive list of unanticipated and nonconforming events that falsify most of Marx's specific theories of history (for more examples, see below).

THE COLLAPSE AND CULTURAL MATERIALISM

Some may conclude that the crisis of Marxism affects the credibility of materialist approaches in general. This is not true, at least for cultural materialism. Indeed, the transformation of the Soviet system has quite a different implication since one of cultural materialism's basic theoretical principles—the primacy of infrastructure—provides a cogent processual framework for understanding the events in question.

As discussed in chapter 11, the infrastructural, structural, and symbolic-ideational features are equally necessary components of human social life, but these sectors do not play a symmetrical role in influencing the retention or extinction of sociocultural innovations. Innovations that arise in infrastructure are likely to be preserved and propagated if they enhance productive and reproductive efficiency under specific environmental conditions—even if there is a marked incompatibility between them and preexisting structural relationships and/or ideologies. Moreover, the resolution of any deep incompatibility between an adaptive infrastructural innovation and the preexisting features of the other sectors will predictably

consist of substantial changes in those other sectors. In contrast, innovations
of a structural or symbolic-ideational nature are likely to be selected against if
there is any deep incompatibility between them and infrastructure.

DECLINING EFFICIENCY OF SOVIET INFRASTRUCTURE

The immediately relevant portion of the principle of the primacy of
infrastructure is that the political-economic (i.e., structural) and
symbolic-ideational innovations introduced in the name of Marxist
materialism resulted in a stagnant, declining, or increasingly inefficient
infrastructure. The Soviet political economy failed because it was incapable of accepting the demise of its smokestack-type infrastructure and
because it inhibited infrastructural innovations for overcoming a deepening technological, demographic, environmental, and economic crisis.

   The general outlines of this failure are well-known, and I shall limit
myself to just a few highlights. On the eve of *perestroika*, in the early 1980s,
the Soviet Union's basic energy supply was in deep trouble (Kuhnert
1991:493). Coal and oil production was stagnant during 1980–1984
(Kuhnert 1991:494). Generating plants and transmission lines were anti-
quated and in a state of disrepair, as manifested in frequent breakdowns
and blackouts (not to mention Chernobyl). In the agricultural sector, grain
production, adjusted for weather conditions, remained about the same in
the 1980s as in the previous decade, despite heavy investment (IMF
1990:138). Two-thirds of agricultural processing equipment in use during
the 1980s was worn out, with much of it dating back to the 1950s and
1960s (IMF 1990:51). From 20 to 50 percent of the grain, potato, sugar
beet, and fruit crops were lost before they got to the store (Goldman
1987:37). Even where supplies were adequate, delays in delivery led to temporary shortages, resulting in long lines, hoarding, and spot rationing.
Between 1970 and 1987, output per unit of input declined at a rate of
more than one percent per year (Gregory and Stuart 1990:147). On the
eve of *perestroika*, there was general agreement from Gorbachev on down
that economic growth per capita was zero or negative (Nove 1989:394).

An even more dismal view of the performance of the Soviet infrastructure emerges when the costs of pollution and environmental depletions are subtracted from the national product. Every conceivable form of pollution and resource depletion existed in life-threatening amounts, including uncontrolled sulfur dioxide emissions, nuclear and other forms of hazardous waste sites, soil erosion, the poisoning of Lake Baikal and the Black, Baltic, and Caspian Seas, and the drying up of the Aral Sea (IMF 1990). It is probably not a coincidence that, as Feshbach (1983) reports, life expectancy for Soviet males also was declining on the eve of *perestroika*.

Moreover, the Soviet Bloc lagged far behind the West in the application of high-tech innovations to the production of nonmilitary goods. By the 1980s, diffusion of technological innovations throughout the economy was taking three times longer in the Soviet Union than in the West (Gregory and Stuart 1990:411), and civilian telecommunications, information processing, and biotechnology remained in a rudimentary state. A telling statistic in this regard is that more than 100,000 villages in the Soviet Union lacked telephone service (IMF 1990:125). The Soviet Union's civilian economy not only lacked computers, but also industrial robots, electronic copiers, optical scanners, and many other information-processing devices that had already become the dominant features of Japanese and Western industrialism fifteen or more years earlier.

STRUCTURAL INCOMPATIBILITIES

How state communism impeded the development of Soviet Bloc infrastructures is also well-known, and I shall assume that a brief summary is sufficient to make the point. A prime source of infrastructural malfunctioning derived from the inherent limitations of the centrally planned and centrally administered command economy and its immense bureaucracy. At the enterprise level, managers were kept under close scrutiny by bureau chiefs in order to assure conformity with a massive list of rules and regulations that had various unintended consequences. The amount of money made available to an enterprise for incentive bonuses was determined

by the number of workers it employed, and this led to the hiring of
large numbers of unneeded workers (IMF 1990:31). Quotas were also
stipulated in crude quantitative terms, resulting in the production of
poor-quality goods. Such quantitative indices were also an invitation
to fulfill quotas by fakery.

> Since salaries, bonuses and promotions depend on achiev-
> ing the plan, the temptation, indeed the pressure, of the
> centrally planned system is to fake the output. (Armstrong
> 1989:24)

A persistent source of inefficiency in the state communist command
structure, described by anthropologist Catherine Verdery (1991:422) for
Eastern Europe, are the "soft budgets" enjoyed by firms and enterprises.
This means that the penalties for inefficient and irrational management,
such as excess inventory, overemployment, and excess investment, were
minimal and did not lead to the extinction of an enterprise. Firms that operated at a loss could always count on subsidies that would bail them out.

> Because of this, and because central plans usually overstate
> productive capacities and raise output targets higher and
> higher each year, firms learn to hoard materials and labor.
> They overstate their material requirements for production,
> and they overstate their investment needs, in hopes of
> having enough to meet or even surpass their assigned
> production targets. (Verdery 1991:422)

These practices locked up productive resources that could have been
put to better use by other enterprises. They contributed to the peculiar
economy of shortages and interminable queuing that beset the Soviet Bloc,
as well as to the hypertrophy of the second, or informal, economy, with its
moonlighting, personalism, and pervasive petty corruption down to "the
clerk who hides goods under the counter for friends and relatives or for a
bribe." (Verdery 1991:423)

The command structure of state communism in general also acted as a drag on technological innovation and on its uptake into the system. The slow pace of technological change reflects in part a general malaise induced by unrelenting pressure to conform to orders from above. More specifically, however, the structure of the command economy lacked sufficient incentives for innovative behavior. There were few rewards for enterprise managers who introduced new and more efficient production processes or products (Berliner 1976; Gregory and Stuart 1990:213). Furthermore, reduction of labor input achieved by improved technologies was unlikely to add to an enterprise's "profits" but would, in conformity with the official labor theory of value, get passed along to the consumer in the form of lower prices (Gregory and Stuart 1990:221).

The command structure of the Soviet Bloc political economy was particularly incompatible with a transition to high-tech industrialism, with its devices that create, store, retrieve, copy, and transmit information at high speeds over national and international networks. The operation of such networks presupposed a large degree of freedom for individuals to exchange information, both vertically and horizontally. It also presumed telephone lines and high-speed switching systems that could handle computer-assisted information flowing in every direction between individuals and organizations.

The Soviet system's command structure, however, was designed to avoid the rapid exchange of information not subject to censorship and party supervision. Indeed, the low priority assigned to the development of a modern telephone network expressed the insecurity of the Communist party more than a lack of technical know-how and resources. The same can be said of the practice of putting locks on the few computers used by civilian enterprises and of making the unauthorized possession of a copying machine a crime against the state.

The Nationalist Surge

If only in passing, permit me to suggest that the general infrastructural debacle also goes a long way toward explaining the nationalist and separatist surge that has led to the breakup of the Soviet empire. The redistributive functions of the center were not only discharged badly, but unevenly. Profound differences in rates of productivity, GNP, damage to the environment, and rates of population growth permeated the USSR. The Central Asian and Transcaucus republics, with their rampant unemployment and decreasing per-capita consumption of meat and dairy products, bore the brunt of the infrastructural crisis. Perhaps the most telling statistic here is that, in the 1970s and 1980s, the level of infant mortality increased in Uzbekistan, Turkmenia, and Kazakhstan by 48, 22, and 14 percent, respectively (Illarianov 1990:9).

Although the least-developed republics received subsidies from the center, the transfers were obviously insufficient. Convinced that the center was taking out more than it was putting in, the republics with the most-developed infrastructures, such as the Baltic group and Ukraine, were convinced that their living standards were being depressed by the center's favoritism toward ethnic Russians and the Russian Republic. They believed that they would advance to Western standards once they were free of the Soviet incubus.

I do not, even in this brief compass, wish to minimize the role of ethnic and linguistic sentiments in mobilizing and sustaining the independence movements. Rather, the point is that these sentiments were not simply sustained by the force of history and tradition, but by the stagnant or deteriorating material circumstances in which people found themselves at a particular moment in their history.

So there you have it: the collapse of the Soviet system and the Soviet empire as a case of selection against a political economy that increasingly impeded and degraded the performance of its infrastructure.

PRIMACY OF INFRASTRUCTURE OR PRIMACY OF POLITICS?

The evidence for concluding that the Soviet Bloc's collapse is an example of the primacy of infrastructure is not as clear-cut as I would like it to be. One could still argue, following Perlo (1991), that the collapse was the consequence of a bad series of leaders who lacked the requisite managerial skills and determination to hold the system together. Indeed, some may wish to advance the thesis that the history of state communism actually disproves the primacy of infrastructure. Since the Soviet command economy lasted for seventy years, the case shows nothing so much as that infrastructure is the dependent variable and that politics are indeed "in command." In rebuttal, I would maintain that the impediments confronted by the Soviet infrastructure did not reach crisis proportions until the 1960s or 1970s. After World War II, Soviet economic growth was still fast enough to lend credence to Nikita Khrushchev's projection that the communist standard of living would exceed that of the United States by 1970 and that capitalism would be buried before the end of the century (Frankland 1967:149–50).

The paradigmatic advantage of the primacy of infrastructure over "politics in command" does not consist simply in the demonstration that, sooner or later, politics that subvert infrastructural performance are selected against. Rather it lies in the additional claim that, under similar infrastructural conditions, structural and symbolic-ideational features evolve along convergent paths, whereas "politics in command" is inherently indifferent to any principled explanation of the direction of change. Thus, the test of the primacy of infrastructure lies not only in the Soviet Bloc's collapse, but in the kinds of societies that will replace the discredited Soviet model.

If the collapse is really nonsystemic and accountable only in terms of individual choice and counterchoice—of the exercise of power and the resistance to power—then the forms of social life that will arise from the ruins of Soviet communism should diverge widely from each other and from the evolving forms of industrial societies everywhere, not excluding the possibility of a return to Leninist-Stalinist regimes. On the other hand, if the collapse is actually part of a process that is bringing the structural and symbolic-ideational components into systemic alignment with post-smokestack industrial infrastructures, then we should expect to see the industrialized Soviet republics and Eastern Europe converging toward systems similar to those emerging in the advanced industrial societies of Europe, Japan, and the United States.

The belief that such a convergence would take place (despite its implications of Marxist determinism [Gellner 1990]) was widely promoted in the West during the 1960s (Kerr 1960; Galbraith 1967; Sorokin 1961; Form 1979) and to a lesser extent in the East (Sakharov 1970). By 1980, however, given the apparently permanent presence of the Soviet Union as an industrial giant and military superpower, the conviction reigned, as much in the East as in the West, that the twain never would meet.

Returning to take a second look at the relationship between political and economic structures and industrialization after twenty years of the Cold War, Clark Kerr concluded that

> industrialism was at least minimally compatible with more
> than a single economic or political structure—with plan
> or with market and with mixtures of the two, and with
> monopoly of and with competition for political power,
> and with mixtures of the two. (1983:74)

On the eve of *perestroika*, it was being said in the West that "such claims [for convergence] seem absurd" (Davis and Scase 1985:5). As late as 1989, a leading reform-minded Soviet economist called convergence a "phantom," insisting that the change in organizational, technological, and managerial relations in the Soviet Union "does not attest to the ... formation of any kind of mixed system" (Shishkov 1989:26). But with elections, privatization, stock markets, "market socialism," and globalization being endorsed throughout the former communist bloc, it is the notion of unblendable systems that has become a phantom.

MARX AGAIN

If Marxism is to maintain any credibility, it must be stripped of most of the theories that lie at the core of its classical canon. But is there anything left to Marxism after one strips away such theoretical ghosts as the implacable miseration of the proletariat, the development of working-class consciousness, the subordination of gender and ethnic interests to class unity, the irreconcilability of class interests, the inevitable triumph of the proletariat, the unblendable natures of capitalism and communism, and the dialectical certainty that communism will replace capitalism? Yes, indeed, for there still remains the fact that the principle of the primacy of infrastructure is a derivative, if substantially modified version of a fundamental part of the classic Marxist paradigm. I cannot refrain from pointing out that Marx's most famous description of the engine of history applies with uncanny precision to what is taking place in the former Soviet Bloc. In the preface to the *Critique of Political Economy*, Marx wrote:

> At a certain stage of development the material productive
> forces of society come into conflict with the existing
> relations of production or—this merely expresses the same
> thing in legal terms—with the property relations within
> the framework of which they have operated hitherto. From
> forms of development of the productive forces these
> relations turn into their fetters. Then begins an era of
> social revolution. (Marx [1859]1970:21)

Marx's formulation of the engine of history has long been mired in the debate over whether he considered the relations of production (or the economic structure) to be separable from productive forces, and whether productive forces possess explanatory primacy over the relations of production. The philosopher G. A. Cohen (1978) has argued persuasively against the more orthodox view that Marx merged the two—productive forces and relations of production—into the "economic foundation" of society. Cohen maintains that Marx accepted the primacy of the forces of production, which he conceived essentially as the primacy of technology.

This interpretation narrows the gap between classical Marxism and cultural materialism, but it still leaves the ecological and demographic aspects of infrastructure in limbo. Moreover, Cohen's depiction of Marx as a technological determinist cannot easily be reconciled with the glaring neglect in *Capital* of technological change as the engine promoting the shift from feudalism to capitalism (Miller 1981). In any event, the singularly ironic fate of Marx's theory of history is that it makes sense only if it is not capitalism, but Soviet-style communism, that acts as the fetter on the productive forces.

A DISCLAIMER

Having examined the relationship between the political economy of state communism and some of the main failings of Soviet Bloc infrastructures, I wish to dissociate myself from the view that the collapse of the Soviet system proves that capitalism is the "end of history" (Fukuyama 1989) or that "capitalism has won":

> History also will credit this year with the victory of Adam
> Smith's political economy over Karl Marx's, the triumph of
> Western capitalism and democracy over Soviet commu-
> nism and dictatorship. (Tobin 1991:5)

Although the malfunctions of neocapitalist systems remain less catastrophic than the malfunctions of the Soviet Bloc, they are nonetheless a source of great instability and pressure for change. Both systems have created life-threatening environmental hazards and depletions; both are plagued by ethnic and racial conflicts; both have severe housing problems; both suffer from bureaucratic hypertrophy; both are riddled with corruption, misinformation, and deception in high places; both have endangered the survival of the species with their nuclear weaponry; and both are prodigiously wasteful of human energy and talent, as can be seen in the recurrent crises of unemployment and overproduction for which capitalism has yet to find a remedy. A system that is so egregiously flawed cannot represent the end-point of history.

It is not merely capitalism's unresolved problems that guarantee the continued evolution of novel sociocultural forms and arrangements in the West as well as in the collapsed Soviet Bloc. Massive changes within the capitalistist infrastructure—associated with declining fertility rates, aging populations, environmental hazards, the expansion of service and information-production, robotization, new computer-assisted design and manufacturing techniques, satellite transmissions, jumbo jets, and bioengineering—have already elicited a new generation of far-ranging modifications in political-economy and symbolic-ideational themes among the leading capitalist countries. These include the unprecedented spread and interpenetration of transnational corporations; the appearance of the firm without a country; the emergence of heteroconsumerism (Colson and Kottak 1990; Levitt 1991) as the world's most popular ideology; the development of supranational trade blocks such as the European Community; and the deepening crisis and uneven development of the former Third World. Anthropology will find it increasingly difficult to justify its existence if it categorically rejects attempts to combine the study of the local microcosm with the study of these and other global phenomena.

The end of history in Fukuyama's essay refers to the triumphant fulfillment of the avowedly Hegelian idea of freedom in the ideology of Western economic and political liberalism. Messy events remain to be worked out (like a nuclear war between Pakistan and India), but to classify events as history "one would have to show that these events were driven by a systematic idea of political and social justice that claimed to supersede liberalism" (Fukuyama 1989, 1990:22). It is difficult to understand why Fukuyama insists that nothing can ever be more rational and free than liberal economics and politics. Anthropologists, idealists as much as materialists, must surely reject this resurrection of Hegel's Eurocentric notions of progress.

~

Finally, it does not follow from the primacy of infrastructure that the material restraints imposed on the rest of social life diminish our freedom to intervene and direct the selection of alternate futures. For along with the restraints come opportunities—opportunities for innovations that can broaden and deepen the benefits of social life for all of humankind. Recognition of the primacy of infrastructure does not diminish the importance of conscious human agency. Rather, it merely increases the importance of having robust theories of history that can guide conscious human choice. If there is one thing that the history of the Soviet bloc demonstrates, it is that conscious interventions and empowerments carried out under the auspices of inadequately developed macro theories of sociocultural evolution readily lead to catastrophic, unintended consequences (Scott 1988). It is true that knowledge is always contested, and it is true that by itself, as so many anthropologists have recently maintained, knowledge does not guarantee freedom; but there can be no freedom without it.

References Cited

Adams, Hunter
1990 African-American Baseline Studies 1990: s-v.

Alexander, Richard
1974 Evolution of social behavior. *Annual Review of Ecological Systems* 5:325–83.

Armstrong, G. Patrick
1989 Gorbachev's nightmare. *Crossroads* 29:21–30.

Barton, C. Michael, and Geoffrey Clark
1997 Evolutionary theory in archaeological perspective. In *Rediscovering Darwin: Evolutionary theory and archaeological exploration*. Archaeological Papers. Arlington, Va.: American Anthropological Association.

Beals, Ralph, and Harry Hoijer
1971 *An introduction to anthropology.* 4th ed. New York: Macmillan.

Beattie, John
1968 Understanding and explanation in social anthropology. In *Theory in anthropology*, edited by R. Manners & D. Kaplan. Chicago: Aldine.

Benedict, Ruth
    1940 *Race: Science and politics.* New York: Modern Age Books.
    1943 *Race and racism.* London: Labour Book Service.

Benedict, Ruth and Mildred Ellis
    1942 *Race and cultural relations: America's answer to the myth of a master race.* Washington, D. C.: National Council for the Social Studies, National Association of Secondary School Principals, National Education Association.

Benedict, Ruth, and Gene Weltfish
    1947 *In Henry's back yard: The races of mankind.* New York: H. Schuman.

Berliner, Joseph S.
    1976 *The innovation decision in Soviet industry.* Cambridge: MIT Press.

Bernal, Martin
    1991 *Black Athena: The Afroasiatic roots of classical civilization.* New Brunswick, N. J.: Rutgers University Press.

Bernard, H. R., P. D. Killworth, D. Kronenfeld, and L. Sailer
    1984. The problem of informant accuracy: The validity of retrospective data. *Annual Review of Anthropology,* 13:495–517.

Beyerchen, Allan
    1993 *What we know about Nazism and science.* Social Research 59:615–41.

Blackburn, Robin, ed.
    1972 *Ideology in social science: Readings in critical social theory.* New York: Vintage.

Boas, Franz
1911 *The mind of primitive man*. New York: Macmillan.

Bohannon, Paul
1963 *Social anthropology*. New York: Holt, Rinehart & Winston.
1973 Rethinking culture: A project for current anthropologists.
Current Anthropology 14:357–72.

Borofsky, Robert, ed.
1994 *Assessing Cultural Anthropology*. New York: McGraw Hill.

Boyd, Robert, and Joan Silk
1997 *How humans evolved*. New York: W. W. Norton.

Brace, Loring
1983 Clines and clusters versus race: A test in Ancient Egypt.
American Journal of Physical Anthropology 36:1–31.
1996 Review of *The Bell Curve*. *Current Anthropology* 37,
supplement:S156–61.

Bradley, Michael
1978 *The iceman inheritance: Prehistoric sources of western man's
racism, sexism, and aggression*. Toronto: Dorset.

Buraway, Michael
1990 Marxism as science: Historical challenges and theoretical
growth. *American Sociological Review* 55:775–93.

Callinicos, Alex
1991 *The revenge of history: Marxism and the East European
revolutions*. Oxford: Polity Press.

Cassidy, C.
  1987 World-view conflict and toddler malnutrition: Change agent
     dilemmas. In *Child survival: Anthropological perspectives on the
     treatment and maltreatment of children*, edited by Nancy
     Scheper-Hughes. Boston: D. Reidel.

Clifford, James, and George Marcus, eds.
  1986 *Writing culture: The poetics and politics of ethnography.*
     Berkeley and Los Angeles: University of California Press.

Cohen, Gerald A.
  1978 *Karl Marx's theory of history: A defense.* Princeton: Princeton
     University Press.
  1988 *History, labour and freedom: Themes from Marx.* New York:
     Oxford University Press.

Collins, Randall
  1989 Sociology: proscience or antiscience? *American Sociological
     Review* 54:124–39.

Colson, Elizabeth, and Conrad Kottak
  1990 Multi-level linkages and longitudinal studies. Paper presented
     at the 89th annual meeting of the American Anthropological
     Association, New Orleans.

Coon, Carleton
  1965 *The living races of man.* New York: Knopf.

D'Andrade, Roy
  1995 Moral models in anthropology. *Current Anthropology*
     36:409ff.

Davenport, Charles
  1912 *Heredity and eugenics.* Chicago: University of Chicago Press.

Davis, Howard, and Richard Scase
1985 *Western capitalism and state socialism: An introduction.* Oxford: Basil Blackwell.

Dawkins, Richard
1976 *The selfish gene.* New York: Oxford University Press.

Dickeman, Mildred
1979 Female infanticide and reproductive strategies of stratified human societies. In *Sociobiology and human social organizations,* edited by Napoleon Chagnon and William Irons. North Scituate, Mass.: Duxbury.

Dixon, Roland
1923 *The racial history of man.* New York: C. Scribner and Sons.

Dobb, M.
1947 Marx on precapitalist economic formations. *Science and Society* 30:319–25.

Draper, Hal
1987 *The "dictatorship of the proletariat" from Marx to Lenin.* New York: Monthly Review.

Duncan, Greg, Jeanne Brooks-Gunn, and Pamela Klebandy
1993 *Economic deprivation and early childhood development.* Ann Arbor: University of Michigan. Photocopy.

Durham, William H.
1991 *Coevolution: Genes culture, and human diversity.* Stanford: Stanford University Press.

Durkheim, Emile
[1893] 1938 *The division of labor in society.* New York: Macmillan.

Edgerton, Robert
    1992 *Sick societies: Challenging the myth of primitive harmony.* New
        York: Free Press.

Ember, Carol, and Melvin Ember
    1990 *Anthropology.* 6th ed. Englewood Ciffs, N. J.: Prentice-Hall.

Executive Committee of the Socialist Party of Great Britain.
    1990 Socialism Has Not Failed. *Socialist Standard* 86 (January):2-6.

Ferguson, B.
    1995 Infrastructural Determinism. In *Science, materialism, and the
        study of culture,* edited by Martin Murphy and Maxine Margolis.
        Gainesville: University Press of Florida.

Feshbach, Murray
    1983 Issues in Soviet health problems. *In Soviet economy in the
        1980s: Problems and prospects.* Selected papers submitted to the
        Joint Economic Committee, Congress of the United States,
        December 31, 1982. Washington, D. C.: Government Printing
        Office.

Form, William
    1979 Comparative industrial sociology and the convergence
        hypothesis. *Annual Review of Sociology* 5:1–25.

Foucault, Michel
    1984 *Foucault reader.* New York: Pantheon.

Frankland, Mark
    1967 *Kruschev.* New York: Stein and Day.

Freeman, Derek
    1983 *Margaret Mead and Samoa: The making and unmaking of an
        anthropological myth.* Cambridge: Harvard University Press.

Fukuyama, Francis

    1989 The end of history? *National Interest* 16(Summer):3–18.

    1990 A Reply to My Critics. *National Interest* 17(Winter):21–8.

Galbraith, John Kenneth

    1967 *The new industrial state.* Boston: Houghton Mifflin.

Galton, Francis

    1908 *Memories of my life.* London: Methuen.

Geertz, Clifford

    1973 *The interpretation of cultures.* New York: Basic Books.

    1976 From the native's point of view: On the nature of anthropological understanding. In *Meaning in anthropology*, edited by K. Basso & H. Selby. Albuquerque: University of New Mexico Press.

    1994 The uses of diversity. In *Assessing cultural anthropology*, edited by Robert Borofsky. New York: McGraw Hill.

Gellner, Ernest

    1990 The theory of history: East and West. *Slavic Review* (April–September):141–150.

Goldman, Marshall I.

    1987 *Gorbachev's challenge: Economic reform in the age of high technology.* New York: W. W. Norton.

Goodenough, Ward

    1964 Cultural anthropology and linguistics. In *Language in culture and society*, edited by Dell Hymes. New York: Harper and Row.

    1965 Rethinking status and role. In *The relevance of models for social anthropology*, edited by M. Banton. New York: Praeger.

Gregory, Paul R., and Robert Stuart
    1990 *Soviet economic structure and performance.* 4th ed. New York: Harper and Row.

Gross, Paul, and Norman Levitt
    1994 *Higher superstition: The academic left and its quarrels with science.* Baltimore: Johns Hopkins Press.

Hames, Raymond
    1992 Time allocation. In *Evolutionary ecology and human behavior,* edited by Eric Alden Smith and Bruce Winterhalder. New York: Aldine De Gruyter.

Harner, M.
    1977 The ecological basis for Aztec sacrifice. *American Ethnologist* 4:117–35.

Harris, Marvin
    1958 *Portugal's African wards.* New York: American Committee on Africa.
    1964 *The nature of cultural things.* New York: Random House.
    1968 *The rise of anthropological theory.* New York: Crowell.
    1975 Why a perfect knowledge of all the rules one must know in order to act like a native cannot lead to a knowledge of how natives act. *Journal of Anthropological Research* 30:242–51.
    1977 *Cannibals and kings: The origins of cultures.* New York: Random House.
    1979 *Cultural materialism: The struggle for a science of culture.* New York: Random House.
    1985 *Good to eat.* New York: Simon and Schuster.
    1989 *Our kind.* New York: Harper and Row.
    1994a Cultural materialism is alive and well and won't go away until something better comes along. In *Assessing cultural anthropology,* edited by Robert Borofsky. New York: McGraw Hill.

1994b *Cultural anthropology*. 4th ed. New York: Harper Collins.

1995 Commentary on articles by Nancy Scheper-Hughes and Roy D'Andrade. *Current Anthropology* 36:423–24.

Harris, Marvin, Gomes Consorte, J. Lang, and B. Byrne
1993 Who are the whites? *Social Forces* 72: 451–62.

Harris, Marvin, and E. Ross, eds.
1987 *Death, sex, and fertility: Population regulation in preindustrial and developing societies*. New York: Columbia University Press.

Haviland, William
1993 *Cultural anthropology*. 7th ed. Orlando: Harcourt Brace Jovanovich.

Hayden, Brian, ed.
1992 *A complex culture of the British Columbia Plateau*. Vancouver: University of British Columbia Press.

Headland, Thomas, K. Pike, and M. Harris, eds.
1990 *Emics and etics: The insider/outsider debate.* Newbury Park, Calif: Sage.

Heilbronner, Robert
1990 The world after communism. *Dissent* (Fall):429–32.

Herrnstein, Richard, and Charles Murray
1995 *The bell curve: Intelligence and class structure in American life*. New York: Free Press.

Hodder, Ian
1982 *Symbols in action. Ethnoarchaeological studies of material culture*. Cambridge: Cambridge University Press.

1985 Postprocessual archaeology. *Advances in Archaeological Method and Theory* 8:1–25.

1986 *Archaeology as long term history.* Cambridge: Cambridge University Press.

1991 Interpretive archaeology and its role. *American Antiquity* 56:7–18.

Hoberman, John

1997 *Darwin's athletes: How sport has damaged Black America and preserved the myth of race.* Boston: Houghton Mifflin.

Hofstadter, Richard

1955 *Social Darwinism in American thought.* Boston: Beacon.

Hollander, Paul

1990 Communism's collapse won't faze the Marxists in academe. *Chronicle of Higher Education* (May 23):A44.

Horgan, John

1995 Get smart, take a test. *Scientific American* (November):12ff.

Howard, Michael, and Janet Dunaif-Hattis

1992 *Anthropology: Understanding human adaptation.* New York: Harper Collins.

Howe, Irving

1990 Some dissenting comments. *Dissent* (Fall):432–5.

Illarianov, A.

1990 Eurasian market. *Twentieth Century and Peace* (June):7–11.

International Monetary Fund

1990 *The economy of the USSR: Summary and recommendations.* Washington, D. C.: World Bank.

Jensen, Arthur
   1969 How much can we boost IQ and scholastic achievement?
   Harvard Educational Review 29:1–123.

Johnson, A.
   1974 Ethnoecology and planting practices in a swidden agricultural
   system. *American Ethnologist* 1:87–101.
   1982 Reductionism in cultural ecology: The Amazon case. *Current
   Anthropology* 23:413–28.

Jones, Eric
   1987 *The European miracle: Environments, economies, and geopolitics
   in the history of Europe and Asia.* New York: Cambridge
   University Press.

Kaplan, Hillard, and Kim Hill
   1992 The evolutionary ecology of food acquisition. In *Evolutionary
   ecology and human behavior,* edited by Eric Alden Smith and
   Bruce Winterhalder. New York: Aldine De Gruyter.

Kamin, Leon J.
   1974 *The science and politics of I.Q.* Potomac, Md: L. Erlebaum.

Keller, Janet
   1992 Schemes for schemata. In *New directions in psychological
   anthropology,* edited by Tim Schwartz, G. White, and C. Lutz.
   New York: Cambridge University Press.

Kennickel, Arthur
   1996 *Weighting design for the 1992 Survey of consumer finances.*
   Washington, D. C.: Federal Reserve.

Kerr, Clark
　1960　*Industrialism and industrial man: The problems of labor and management in economic growth.* Cambridge, Mass.: Harvard University Press.
　1983　*The future of industrial societies: Covergence or continuing diversity?* Cambridge, Mass.: Harvard University Press.

Kochar, V. K.
　1976　Human factors in the regulation of parasitic infections. In *Medical Anthropology,* edited by F. Grollig and H. Halley. The Hague: Mouton.

Kolakowski, L.
　1978　*Main currents of Marxism: Its origins, growth and dissolution.* New York: Oxford University Press.

Kottak, Conrad
　1991　*Cultural Anthropology.* 5th ed. New York: McGraw Hill.

Kroeber, Alfred
　1948　*Anthropology.* New York: Harcourt Brace.

Kroeber, Alfred, and Talcott Parsons
　1958　The concept of culture and of social systems. *American Sociological Review* 23: 582–3.

Kuhnert, Caroline.
　1991　More power for the Soviets: Perestroika and energy. *Soviet Studies* 43(3): 491–506.

Kuznar, Lawrence
　1997　*Reclaiming a scientific anthropology.* Walnut Creek, Calif.: AltaMira.

Lesser, Alexander
　　1981 Franz Boas. In *Totems and teachers: Perspectives on the history of anthropology*, edited by Sydel Silverman. New York: Columbia University Press.

Levine, Nancy
　　1988 *The dynamics of polyandry*. Chicago: University of Chicago Press.

Levi-Strauss, Claude
　　1972 Structuralism and ecology. *Barnard Alumnae* (spring):6–14. [Reprinted in *Readings in Anthropology*, edited by A. Weiss. Guilford, Conn.: Dushkin.]

Levitt, Theodore
　　1991 *Thinking about management*. New York: Free Press.

Lieberman, Leonard, and Rodney Kirk
　　1997 Teaching about human variation: An anthropological tradition for the twenty-first century. In *The teaching of anthropology: Problems, issues, and decisions*, edited by Conrad Kottak, Jane White, Pat Rice, and Richard Furlow. Mountain View, Calif.: Mayfield.

Lowie, Robert
　　1920 *Primitive society*. New York: Boni and Leveright.
　　1937 *History of ethnological theory*. New York: Farrar and Rinehart.

Mannheim, Karl
　　1936 *Ideology and utopia*. New York: Harcourt Brace.

Marano, L.
　　1982 Windigo psychosis: The anatomy of an emic-etic confusion. *Current Anthropology* 23:385–412.

Marcus, G., and M. Fischer
    1986 *Anthropology as cultural critique.* Chicago: University of
    Chicago Press.

Margolis, Maxine, and Martin Murphy, eds.
    1995 *Science, materialism, and the study of culture.* Gainesville:
    University Press of Florida.

Marx, Karl
    [1859] 1970 *A contribution to the critique of political economy.* New
    York: International Publishers.

Mead, Margaret
    1928 *Coming of age in Samoa.* New York: W. Morrow.
    1942 *And keep your powder dry.* New York: W. Morrow.

Miller, Barbara
    1981 *The endangered sex.* Ithaca, N. Y.: Cornell University Press.

Molnar, Stephen
    1983 *Human variation: Races, types, and ethnic groups.* Englewood
    Cliffs, N. J.: Prentice-Hall.
    1992 *Human variation: Races, types, and ethnic groups.* 3rd ed.
    Englewood Cliffs, N. J.: Prentice-Hall.

Montagu, Ashley
    1950 *Statement on race: An extended discussion in plain language of
    the UNESCO statement by experts on race problems.* New York:
    Schuman.

Moore, John
    1994 Ethnogenetic theories. *National Geographic Research and
    Exploration* 10:10–23.

Mulder, Monique Borgerhoff
  1992 Reproductive decisions. In *Evolutionary ecology and human behavior*, edited by Eric Alden Smith and Bruce Winterhalder. New York: Aldine De Gruyter.

Nanda, Serena
  1991 *Cultural anthropology*. 4th ed. Belmont, Calif.: Wadsworth.

Neisser, Ulrich, ed.
  1998 *The rising curve: Long term gains in IQ and related measures*. Washington, D. C.: American Psychological Association.

Niebuhr, R. Gustav
  1991 Fatima fever: Did Mary prophesy Soviet goings-on? *Wall Street Journal* (September 27):p.1.

Nove, Alec
  1989 *An economic history of the USSR*. London: Penguin Books.

Obeyesekere, Gananath
  1992 *The apotheosis of Captain Cook: European mythmaking in the Pacific*. Princeton, N. J.: Princeton University Press.

O'Meara, Tim
  1997 Causation and the struggle for a science of culture. *Current Anthropology* 38(3): 399–418.

Oppenheimer, Valerie
  1982 *Work and the family: A study in social demography*. New York: Academic Press.

Ortiz de Montellano, Bernard
  1993 Melanin, Afrocentricity, and pseudo-science. *Yearbook of Physical Anthropology* 36: 33–58.

Paredes, Anthony
  1997 Race is not something that you can see. *Anthropology Newsletter* 38 (9):1ff.

Parsons, Talcott
  1961 An outline of the social system. In *Theories of society*, edited by Talcott Parsons. Glencoe, Ill.: Free Press.

Perlo, Victor
  1991 The economic and political crisis in the USSR. *Political Affairs* 70 (August): 10–18.

Pike, K. L.
  1954, 1955, 1960 *Language in relation to a unified theory of the structure of human behavior.* 3 vols. Glendale, Calif.: Summer Institute of Linguistics.
  1986a Mixtec social "credit rating": The particular versus the universal in one emic world view. *Proceedings of the National Academy of Sciences* 83:3047–304.
  1986b Personal communication. Letter, 24 June.

Price, David
  1994 Wittfogel's neglected hydraulic/hydroagricultural distinction. *Journal of Anthropological Research* 50:44–54.
  1996 *Cold War anthropology: Collaborators and victims of the national security state.* Unpublished.

Rappaport, R.
  1984 *Pigs for the ancestors: Ritual in the ecology of a New Guinea people.* 2d ed. New Haven: Yale University Press.

Reyna, Stephen P.
  1994 Literary anthropology and the case against science. *Man* 29:555–82.

Robarchek, Clayton
1989 Primitive warfare and the ratomorphic view of mankind. *American Anthropologist* 91:903–20.

Rogers, Alan
1992 Resources and population dynamics. In *Evolutionary ecology and human behavior*, edited by Eric Alden Smith and Bruce Winterhalder. New York: Aldine De Gruyter.

Rosenau, Pauline
1992 *Post-modernism and the social sciences: Insights, inroads, and intrusions*. Princeton, N. J.: Princeton University Press.

Rosenberg, Alfred
[1930] 1970 *Race and race history, and other essays*. New York: Harper and Row.

Sacks, Karen
1994 How did Jews become white folks? In *Race*, edited by Steven Gregory and Roger Sanjek. Rutgers, N. J.: Rutgers University Press.

Sahlins, Marshall
1995 *How "natives" think: About Captain Cook, for example.* Chicago: University of Chicago Press.

Sakharov, Andrei
1970 *Progress, coexistence, intellectual freedom*. New York: W. W. Norton.

Sanderson, Stephen
1990 *Social evolutionism: a critical history*. Oxford: Basil Blackwell.
1991 *Macrosociology*. New York: Harper Collins.
1994 The transition from feudalism to capitalism: The theoretical significance of the Japanese case. *Fernand Braudel Center Review* 17:15–55.

Sanjek, Roger
   1990 *Fieldnotes: The making of anthropology.* Ithaca, N. Y.: Cornell
       University Press.

Sapir, Edward
   1921 *Language: An introduction to the study of speech.* New York:
       Harcourt Brace.

Scarr, Sandra, and Richard Weinberg
   1976 IQ test performance of black children adopted by white
       families. *American Psychologist* 31:726–39.

Scheper-Hughes, Nancy
   1995 The primacy of the ethical: Propositions for a militant
       anthropology. *Current Anthropology* 36:409ff.
   1987 Culture, scarcity, and maternal thinking: Mother love and
       child death in northeast Brazil. In *Child survival: Anthropological
       perspectives on the treatment and maltreatment of children,* edited
       by Nancy Scheper-Hughes. Boston: D. Reidel.

Schiffer, M.
   1983 Review of cultural materialism. *American Antiquity* 48:190–94.

Schlegel, Alice, and Herbert Barry
   1991 *Adolescence: An anthropological inquiry.* New York: Free Press.

Schlesinger, Arthur
   1992 *The disuniting of America.* New York: W. W. Norton.

Scott, James
   1998 *Seeing like a state: How certain schemes to improve the human
       condition have failed.* New Haven: Yale University Press.

Scrimshaw, S.
1984 Infanticide in human populations: Societal and individual concerns. *In Infanticide: Comparative and evolutionary perspectives*, edited by G. Hausfater & S. Hrdy. New York: Aldine.

Sebring, J.
1987 Bovidicy. *Journal of Anthropological Research* 43:398–419.

Shanklin, Eugenia
1994 *Anthropology and race*. Belmont, Calif.: Wadsworth.

Shankman, Paul
1996 The history of Samoan sexual conduct and the Mead-Freeman controversy. *American Anthropologist* 98:555–67.

Shanks, Michael, and Christopher Tilley
1987 *Reconstructing archaeology*. Cambridge: Cambridge University Press.

Shishkov, I. V.
1989 Peristroika and the phantom of convergence. *Problems of Economics* 32:6–28.

Sidky, H.
1996 *Irrigation and state formation in Hunza: The anthropology of a hydraulic kingdom*. Boston: University Press of America.

Skinner, B. F.
1984 Selection by consequences. *Behavioral and Brain Sciences* 7:477–510.

Smith, Eric Alden, and Bruce Winterhalder, eds.
1992 *Evolutionary ecology and human behavior*. New York: Aldine De Gruyter.

Smith, Thomas
1966 *The agrarian origins of modern Japan.* New York: Atheneum.

Sorokin, P. A.
1961 *Mutual convergence of the United States and the USSR to the mixed sociological type.* Mexico City: Costa-Amic.

Spencer, Herbert
1896 [1876] *Principles of sociology.* New York: D. Appleton.

Stearns, Peter, Michael Adas, and Stuart Schwartz
1992 *World Civilizations.* New York: Harper Collins.

Stoskopf, Allan
1996 Confronting the forgotten history of the American eugenics movement. *Facing History and Ourselves News.* pp.3 ff.

Strathern, Marilyn
1987 Out of context: The persuasive fiction of anthropology. *Current Anthropology* 8:251–81.

Tobin, James
1991 The Adam Smith address. *Business Economics* 26(1):5–17.

Van Beek, W. E. A.
1991 Dogon restudies: A field evaluation of the work of Marcel Griault. *Current Anthropology* 12:139–67.

Verdery, Katherine
1991 Theorizing socialism: A prologue to the "Transition." *American Ethnologist* 18:419–39.

Vining, Daniel
   1985 Social versus reproductive success: The central theoretic
      problem of sociobiology. *Behavioral and Brain Sciences* 9:167–
      216.

Wallerstein, Immanuel
   1974 *The modern world systems: Capitalist agriculture and the origins
      of the European world economy in the sixteenth century.* New
      York: Academic.

Wallich, Paul, and Elizabeth Corcoran
   1991 The analytical economist: Don't write off Marx. *Scientific
      American* 264(2): 135.

Watson, Richard
   1990 Ozymandias, king of kings: Postprocessual radical archaeology
      as critique. *American Antiquity* 55:673–89.

Weber, Max
   [1904] 1958 *The Protestant ethic and the spirit of capitalism.* New
      York: Charles Scribners.

Weinberg, Richard, Sandra Scarr, and Irwin Waldman
   1992 The Minnesota transracial adoption study: A follow-up of IQ
      test performance at adolescence. *Intelligence* 16:117ff.

Welsing, Francis
   1991 *The Isis (Yssis) papers.* Chicago: Third World Press.

Werner, Oswald
   1973 Structural anthropology. In *Main currents in anthropology,*
      edited by R. Naroll and F. Naroll. New York: Appleton-Century-
      Crofts.

Wittfogel, Karl
    1957 *Oriental despotism*. New Haven: Yale University Press.

Yurco, Frank
    1989 Unconscious of race: Were the Ancient Egyptians black or
        white? *Biblical Archaeology Review* 15(5):24–9.

Index

Page numbers set in italics indicate references cited in the text.

religion, and rise of capitalism, 165
replication, 158–9
reproduction, biological, 108
reproduction, human
    and evolutionary fitness, 68,
        103–4, 107
    financial status, effect on, 100–02
    interbreeding within, 75
    measurability of, 102–4
research, political-moral choices in, 59
Reyna, Stephen P., 61, 160
Robarchek, Clayton, *137–8*
Rogers, Alan, on human reproduc-
        tion, 101
Rome, 164–5
Rosenau, Pauline, *64, 154*, 155–6
Rosenberg, Alfred, 129
Ross, E., 166

S

Sacks, Karen, 71
sacred cow complex, 44–5
Sahlins, Marshall, 38, 39
Sailer, L., *40*
Sakharov, Andrei, *186*
Samoa, 70–1
San (Botswana), 104
Sanderson, Stephen, on capitalism, 163,
        165, 166–71
Sanjek, Roger, *158*
Sapir, Edward, on "primitive"
        language, 70
Scarr, Sandra, 94–5
Scase, Richard, 186
Scheper-Hughes, Nancy
    on critical anthropology, 62–5, 85

on infanticide, 46–7
Schlegel, Alice, 70
Schlesinger, Arthur, *127*
Schwartz, Stuart, *164–5*, 173
science
    as dehumanizing, 155
    empirical, 52–3
    and morality, 58–60
    and politics, 60–1
    postmodern attacks on, 58, 153,
        154–5
    See also emics; etics; replication
Scott, James, 190
Scrimshaw, S., *47*
Sebring, J., on cattle rearing, 45
selection
    by consequence, 145–7, 151
    cultural, 100–02
    natural, 127–8
    See also Boasians; neo-Darwinism
Shanklin, Eugenia, *73*
Shankman, Paul, 70
Shanks, Michael, *42*
Shishkov, I. V., 186
Shockley, William, 96
Shuey, Audrey, 96
Sick Societies (Edgerton), 145
Silk, Joan, 102
Skinner, B. F., 144
slavery
    in Africa, development of, 115, 122
    in ancient world, 164–5
    and capitalism, 165
Smith, Adam, 50
Smith, Bruce, 99
Smith, Eric Alden, *99, 103, 104*